W9-AAV-058

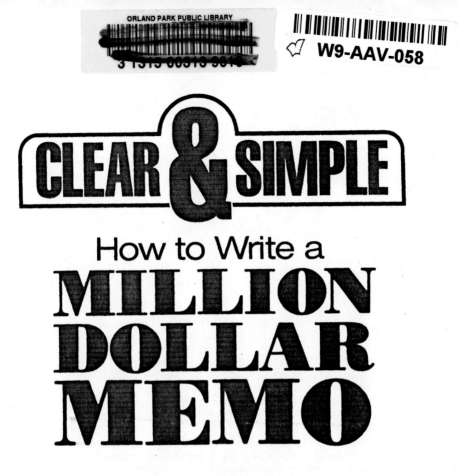

CLEAR & SIMPLE

How to Write a

MILLION DOLLAR MEMO

Cheryl Reimold

A DELL TRADE PAPERBACK

A DELL TRADE PAPERBACK
Published by
Dell Publishing Co., Inc.
1 Dag Hammarskjold Plaza
New York, New York 10017

Copyright © 1984 by Cheryl Reimold and Cloverdale Press, Inc.
Produced by Cloverdale Press, 133 Fifth Avenue, New York, N.Y. 10003

Dell ® TM 681510, Dell Publishing Co., Inc.

Printed in the United States of America

Library of Congress Cataloging in Publication Data

Reimold, Cheryl.
How to write a million dollar memo.

(Clear & simple: a rapid access management primer for young professionals)
1. Memorandums.   I. Title.
HF5726.R423   1984   651.7′55   83-19011
ISBN 0-440-53782-7

Cover design by David M. Nehila

Anyone can make history.
Only a great man can write it.
Oscar Wilde

I am a Bear of Very Little Brain,
and long words Bother me.
A. A. Milne

To my father

Contents

Preface

You are a writer. Have you ever thought of yourself that way? Whatever your title or professional expertise, you spend some part of every day writing. That's how you reach other people both inside and outside your organization. That's how you show them who you are, what you're doing, and why *you* are the best at doing it.

Your writing can make your career. It can persuade people to do what you want them to do. Or—it can turn your readers off.

This book will show you how to make your writing work for, not against, you. There is no middle path. People will be either intrigued or bored, impressed or untouched, eager to work with you or uninterested in your proposal. It's up to you. *You* can determine how they react, simply by the way you write.

What constitutes a great memo? It's persuasive. It's interesting. It's informative. This book shows you how to be all three—and more.

You'll learn how to write clear and simple memos, letters, proposals, and reports. In the interests of clear and simple writing, I have adopted one pronoun for both sexes. When you read "he," think "he/she." We all know I am referring to both, so why make an unreadable fuss about it?

Let's just keep it simple—that's lesson number one.

Introduction

Anyone in business who wants to make money—and that means *anyone* in business—needs to master one vital skill. He must be able to use language effectively. Period.

Think about it. Today, more than ever before, you have to be able to write and speak cogently to:

• Get a job. Competing with the hordes of the skilled unemployed today, you need an attention-grabbing letter and resume just to get an interview.

• Get a promotion. Technical expertise is *not* enough. Those who wish to rise within the corporate ranks must show their ability to manage a staff *and* to keep their superiors informed by means of clear, effective communication.

• Get corporate funding for your program. As industrial technology becomes more specialized and complex, technical memos and reports can sound more and more like gibberish to the company executives who read them.

• Get your work done—whoever you are. Secretaries must regularly read letters, answer them, and even sign them. Managers can spend hours sitting at their desks trying to draft memos, letters, or reports. Doctors, lawyers, politicians, computer scientists—they all have to write memos, proposals, sometimes even speeches, day after day after day.

This book will help you improve your work and increase your prospects through effective use of language. Effective writing is writing that *gets you what you want*. A job. A raise. A promotion. Money for your project. You'll see how you can accomplish these dreams, just by learning how to write a good memorandum. You'll discover how to apply the million-dollar memo technique to job application letters, letters of complaint, and technical memos and reports—all with the same effective results.

In the following pages, you'll learn a new way of thinking and a new way of writing. You will find specific techniques for every stage of writing, and suggestions on whether to write on paper or to dictate. You'll see how a word processor fits beautifully into the million-dollar method. There are tips on the appearance and format of a memo and guidelines for interesting beginnings and useful endings. You'll even find self-help exercises.

What you *won't* find is a selection of memo forms for you to copy and fill in, which is exactly what businesspeople have been doing for decades—pulling out stock forms and filling them in with more anonymous information. A memo, like every other piece of writing, should be a sincere

viii

expression of thought from you to another person. Personal communication has nothing to do with filling in forms—as you will see.

The 1980s could easily be called "The Age of Communication." Our specialties and professions are diverse, isolated, and insulated—yet they are so very interdependent that without a good, clear *lingua franca* to tell each other what we're doing, we'd be going back to the Tower of Babel. Business today is desperate for a key to communication. It cannot function without it.

The key is here—for you.

PART I

THE MILLION-DOLLAR MEMO

A powerful agent is the right word.
Mark Twain

Writing, when properly managed ...
is but a different name for conversation.
Laurence Sterne

1   The Secret of the Million-Dollar Memo

A million-dollar memo is a memo that gets you what you want. It does so by filling your reader's need for readable, understandable communication.

The core of the million-dollar memo is *willingness*—willingness to extend yourself, to give something of yourself. If you've got the willingness inside and this book in your hand, you can write a million-dollar memo.

First, let's look at those million dollars. You may not realize how close they already are. If you've got a $25,000-a-year job and can expect annual raises of ten percent, you'll make your million in less than 17 years. If you're making $20,000, you'll have made a million in less than 19 years. A million dollars is *not* just a dream.

But—maybe you don't feel like waiting so long for it. Maybe you'd like to get on the fast track. An executive making $65,000 a year will make his million in less than ten years. That's with a ten percent yearly increase, and it doesn't include benefits.

So a million dollars is not out of your reach. It's real, it's there, and you can make it faster than you thought possible *by learning to write well.*

Why? Because if you write well, people will read, hear, and listen to you. Because you'll be one of those very *few* people in business whose memos, letters, and reports will be a pleasure to receive. Because you will be answering the crying need for clear, simple communication.

Think of the hours you spend every day trying to decipher the verbose pieces of "information" that cross your desk. Now imagine your boss's reading load! The more people reporting to you, the more memos you get. The more memos you get, the less time you have to read each one. And you will commend only the ones that tell you clearly and simply what you want to know, the ones that fill your needs.

You bought this book because you hoped it would fill your need to get closer to a million dollars—or whatever other goal it is that motivates you. The only reason we read anything is to fill a specific need, whether it's aesthetic or practical. *And the people we value most highly are those who fill our most important needs.*

Good communication is one of the most important needs of all businesses. Indeed, it is the lifeblood of a corporation. Without it, all the financial geniuses in the world couldn't bring a company success.

If you look carefully at the top managers in your company, you'll see that they didn't get where they are on technical expertise alone.

To make the kind of decisions that will help yield hefty profits, top management has to know and understand exactly what is going on in all the company's departments, from accounting to research and development. Similarly, every department head needs to know his staff's ideas, proposals, ambitions, and problems, if the department is to be productive and well run. And each manager must be able to communicate well with his staff. Otherwise, they might misunderstand directions, take offense, or not function well in general.

So—the million-dollar memo is the one that gets you what you want by filling your readers' needs. It's clear and simple. And this book will show you how to write it. All you have to provide is the willingness to try.

HOW TO COMMUNICATE — NOT JUST INFORM

Now let's look at that word *communication*. It stems from the Latin word *communis*, which means "common." It has to do with what is common to all of us—our humanity, if you will.

To communicate means far more than *to inform*. Yet too often in business we confuse the two. We *inform* people of the facts as we know them, and consider that we have *communicated* with them—and wonder why we don't get more response.

The informer provides data, period. The word has even acquired sinister overtones, as we think of police "informers," foreign agent "informers." Perhaps the word became apt for such officers precisely because it suggests a lack of humanity. An encyclopedia can inform, a data sheet can inform, a computer can inform. But only a human being can communicate.

And the great communicators are those who reach out into the common ground of humanity and seek to touch as many human needs as possible. Not just the need to know, or "be informed," but other equally powerful needs that propel us to work, to play, to make decisions, to choose one method over another—to promote one person over another. Communication touches all those needs.

HOW TO FIND—AND FILL— YOUR READER'S NEEDS

The good communicator determines to answer as many of these human needs as possible. And people respond, rewarding the communicator with an effort to meet *his* needs.

What are these needs? I'll give you my list in a minute, and you will no doubt unearth more yourself. Think about yourself for a moment. Why do you work? Yes, for money, that famous million dollars that'll be yours sooner than you think. But is that all? Are you in business only for money?

2

Or is there something in your job, in the profession you've chosen, that you really enjoy, for its own sake? Something that fills a need, makes your day exciting, worthwhile, something to think about and talk about when the workday is over? Something that's maybe worth even more than a million dollars?

Suppose you had that million dollars right now. What would you do—after you'd returned from your cruise to the Bahamas? After you'd invested the money, with a 30 percent return? After you'd ensured that you'd never have to work again, for money? Would you just take another cruise . . . and then another . . . and then another?

Probably not. If you're reading this book, chances are you're someone who is highly motivated, who loves to learn to do things well . . . effectively . . . profitably—even just for their own sake. What else do you like to do?

What are *your* needs?

Stop a minute and take out a sheet of paper. Write down all the things you would do if you had that million dollars. Then, next to each one, write down why.

Your whys will give you a list of your most important needs. Perhaps they include:

companionship

approval

the pleasure of a job well done

mental stimulation

discovery and broadening of your knowledge

aesthetic satisfaction

Those are some of my needs, honestly stated. You may share some and add others. Together, our list probably comprises most of the needs we have as human beings, needs whose fulfillment helps make our life complete and enjoyable.

Remember: the million-dollar memo is the memo that gets you what you want.

The secret of the million-dollar memo is to fill the needs of your readers.

Then they will try to give you what you want.

Now, how do you go about answering all these deep human needs in a simple, practical business memo?

You start by being aware of the needs and trying hard to fill them. Most people never even get that far; they're too focused on *informing* to think about *communicating*. Then you consider each need on your list.

Companionship. You will write a friendly, personal memo that suggests a smile and a handshake, not a computational buzz. You'll use the language and the tone you would use when speaking to a friend. You will let your personality show through and share it with your readers.

Approval. You will approach your readers with respect, making them feel that you honestly care about their response and value their opinion.

The pleasure of a job well done. You will write a memo that is complete, understandable, and reasonable. If you have a suggestion to make, show your readers that it will indeed help *them* in *their* work (not just you in yours).

Mental stimulation. Assume your readers want to be stimulated. Share the excitement of your findings or proposals with them. If you're writing about something that interests them—as you should be—assume they're willing to put some effort into thinking about and understanding it, and give them the information they need to do so.

Discovery and broadening of your knowledge. Like you, your readers want to know more, especially about things that affect them and their work. Tell them—but in clear, simple language that they don't have to decipher. Give them the background knowledge they need to understand what you're about to tell them. Write coherently and logically. Don't worry—you'll learn *how* to do all this in the following chapters!

Aesthetic satisfaction. Make your memo a pleasure to read. Use words with care. Don't keep hammering away at the same sentence structure. Don't overfill your page or your paragraphs. Read it over to hear if it *sounds* good to you.

The way you will go about filling these and other needs is the subject of this book. For now, just concentrate on remembering that *you will try to fill them* every time you write anything to anyone.

That's your million-dollar memo secret.

WHAT'S SO IMPORTANT ABOUT A MEMO?

If communication is the lifeblood of a corporation, memos are the circulation. They are the means by which people all over the company speak to each other, on paper. Every time you write a memo you have the unique chance to make a number of significant people in the company think well of you. Indeed, your memos may be the only exposure you get to certain members of top management, for a while at least. In your memos, you show your superiors your character, your professional strengths, your creative solutions, and your ability to express your ideas clearly and effectively. The memo is your daily million-dollar tool.

Also, if you can write a good memo, you can write anything in business. The memo is the ultimate challenge. It's a letter—but it goes to

4

more than one reader, so you have to consider a multiplicity of interests and needs. It's a report—but it's much shorter than a standard one, so you have to compress your story without making it appear incomplete or densely unreadable. It's often a piece of technical information—but it's usually sent to nontechnical people, so you must be sure to be clear, explicit, *and* interesting.

The rules for writing a million-dollar memo apply to all the notes, letters, reports, and papers you'll ever write. In the following chapters, you'll learn how to adapt them to each specific need.

2 Changing Your Approach

Let's take a look at a typical memo. Say you attended a conference on techniques of management and are writing a memo describing it to your boss and a few other influential people in the company. First, we'll consider the *old* way of doing it — the way most people in business sadly still approach memo-writing today.

TO WRITE A MEMO: THE OLD WAY

1. Don the business-writing attire—figuratively. Notice I didn't say, "Put on your business clothes." That wouldn't be business language! The idea is to feel important, a little stuffy, and at the same time slightly obsequious to your superiors. Whatever you feel, make sure it's polysyllabic—just like the words you're about to use in your memo.

2. Fill in the heading

TO: SUBJECT:

FROM: DATE:

with a minimum of information. After SUBJECT: just write "XYZ Conference, April 5, 1983."

3. Begin by announcing what you're writing about, using as many words as possible, preferably in the passive voice. For example:

> On April 5, 1983, a trip was made by B. Shore and J. Abrams to Appleton, Wisconsin, for the purpose of attending the XYZ Conference on Management Techniques. The scope and subject areas covered by the XYZ Conference are described herein.

4. Go through the conference chronologically—from the first lecture you attended to the last, giving a general idea of each topic discussed.

5. Close by mentioning that the traffic control techniques suggested in one lecture sounded worth trying—but say so in an impersonal, hedging way:

> It appeared to the participants from this corporation that certain of the "traffic control techniques" outlined by M. Barker of the Brass Band Corporation might conceivably be of limited value to this company, provided they were studied in detail and adapted to suit the company's particular exigencies.

6. Append a resume of each speech or session. Failing that, add a summary of those that interested you.

Does this outlined memo look familiar? It should. It is simply a replica of several actual "trip memos" I have before me, from different people in different companies. Each reflects diligent, hard work on the part of the writer, both in active attendance at the conference and in a determined effort to produce a complete, useful memo from it.

But for all the writer's hard work, this "typical memo" is a disaster. It's boring. It gets tied up in its own puffy polysyllabics. It doesn't look as if a real person wrote it: it could have been conceived and produced by a computer. And the response it is likely to elicit from the writer's boss is a check mark by his name and a note to his secretary to put it in the files, thereby "completing" the XYZ Conference project. It is very unlikely that the reader will be inspired to consider implementing any of M. Barker's traffic control techniques. He probably didn't get far enough down the sheet to read about them.

Now let's have a look at another approach to the XYZ Conference memo.

TO WRITE A MEMO: THE NEW WAY

1. Put on your most comfortable clothes, pull up a chair, and sit down for a chat—figuratively. Have you ever watched the television program *Mister Rogers' Neighborhood,* with a pre-schooler? If not, do so soon. You'll learn a lot about simple, honest language for communication—the only good language there is. The program invariably opens with Fred Rogers coming through the front door, then exchanging his coat for his sweater and his street shoes for his sneakers. Relaxed and feeling at home, he sits down to talk to *one* child—the child who's watching him on TV. That's the image you should have of yourself when you start to write anything. You're sitting down comfortably to talk to one other person, simply and honestly.

2. Begin *talking,* in your mind. Set up a dialogue with one of the people to whom the memo is addressed—the one whose reaction means most to you. Put yourself in that person's position. Consider his interests, priorities, wants, needs, character, present state of mind. Be ready to write down the dialogue *exactly* as you hear it in your mind. You're much more likely to speak in lively, expressive language. We tend to save the ponderous pomposities for our writing.

3. Once you've got past the embarrassment of "hearing voices," get the dialogue going and write it down. It consists of questions by your prospective reader and answers by you. Your answers will form the substance of your memo.

The dialogue on the XYZ Conference memo might run as follows:

You: I have something to tell you.

Reader: What is it?

You: It's about the Conference on Management Techniques that Bill Shore and I attended on April 5th.

Reader: Oh yes. Well, I'm pretty busy right now. Was there anything in the conference that would really interest me?

You: Yes, indeed. Mike Barker described a new way of controlling traffic that I think could save us a lot of time and irritation in this department — particularly. during times of heavy deliveries. Barker is Vice President of Sales at the Brass Band Corporation.

Reader: What does Barker suggest? [*Tell him — in a couple of sentences.*]

Reader: That sounds like something that really might work for us. Was there anything else that we could use?

You: *(if the conference was enlightening):* The choice of topics shows that management training is going in a certain direction. [*Explain how, briefly.*]

You: *(if there were a few other good talks).* Two other talks were interesting. [*Say why, briefly.*]

You: *(if there was nothing else worth taking the reader's time to note):* Other than Barker's talk, the conference was routine. I do have a summary of each talk, though, in case you'd like to read them for yourself.

Reader: Thank you very much. I'm glad you went to that conference. You've certainly extracted all the good material for us. That was a first-class job.

---

4. Now—write your memo. Use your first answer to fill in the identifying information at the head. Make your "SUBJECT" entry *complete,* so you don't have to repeat it in the text. Instead of "XYZ Conference, April 5, 1983," as in the old-style memo, write what you said in answer to the reader's first question:

J. Abrams and B. Shore's report on the XYZ Conference on Management Techniques, held in Appleton, Wisconsin, April 5, 1983.

Now you don't have to waste that crucial first paragraph telling your reader the details of what he's already gathered from the heading.

Instead, you use the first paragraph *to get the reader's interest.* That means you answer his needs or questions first, right up front. Never mind the chronological order of the conference doings. Go back to your dialogue and begin your memo with your answer to the reader's main question, "Was there anything that would really interest *me?*"

In this memo, you begin with M. Barker's great ideas for traffic control. Tell your reader succinctly what Barker's technique is and how it might save your company time and irritation.

If there is anything else of interest to any of your readers, tell them in the next two or three paragraphs. (Go back to your last answer in the dialogue.) If not, give a very brief summary of the conference and add your list of summaries as a separate sheet.

As you gain practice in the new way of writing, you will be able to keep your dialogues in your head without writing them down. But don't start out that way. Your first lesson in writing a million-dollar memo is to write *clear and simple language*—and the best place to start looking for that is in your own natural, uninhibited speech.

THE "NEED" TEST

To see how well these two memos rank as pieces of human communication, we can match them against the list of needs.

Companionship. The first memo was written by a nonperson—or a person trying to simulate an anonymous producer of business bafflegab. The writer made every attempt possible not to let his personality show through. In the second memo, the writer was trying to create a companionable meeting on paper. He was literally speaking to the reader, imagining the reader was there with him. The reader would feel that personal act of reaching out to him.

Approval. The reader of the old memo would hardly feel that his opinion was of great import to the writer. All he has before him is a chronological list of events. But the new memo implies, from the beginning, "I value you. That's why I'm telling you what *you* will be interested to hear, first. I want to meet your needs—you're worth it."

Pleasure of a job well done. In no way does the old memo speak to this need. Drab and lifeless itself, *it* is not a job particularly well done. It doesn't give the reader any conviction that it will help him get *his* done well. But memo number two does both. In its presentation of the conference from the point of view of the reader's interests, it makes the reader feel that the writer did a first-class job as company representative there. And in its enthusiastic, complete discussion of the traffic control techniques, it shows the reader a way to get his own job done better.

Mental stimulation. This one's easy. Memo number one gives the reader nothing to think about, unless he reads diligently to the last line. Even then, the hedging suggestion that the traffic control techniques might be worth considering is unlikely to light any cerebral fires. Memo number two has offered a solution to an irritating problem and has possibly added some further interesting insights gained at the conference. It starts the reader thinking.

Discovery and broadening of knowledge. Memo number one gives the reader information. Memo number two turns that information into knowledge, as the writer *discovers* the possible ramifications for the company in the conference deliberations and tells the reader why the material might be interesting.

Aesthetic satisfaction. The old memo is a dull, shapeless bore. The new one flows with natural speech and takes on the form of a satisfying conversation, as it answers the reader's unspoken questions as they arise.

Simple as it is, memo number two passes the million-dollar test. By filling the reader's needs, it gets you what you want: complete attention, approval by influential people, and a good chance that your suggestion will be tried.

It's a million-dollar memo.

3 The Mechanics of Making a Memo

A million-dollar memo is the result of careful planning, from the moment of conception to the final typing or printing. Before we consider the writing techniques, let's look at the printed page. Is it more effective to write or dictate it? Can you produce a million-dollar memo on a word processor? And how should you set up your memo to give it the greatest visual appeal? We'll look at the pros and cons of writing, dictating, and word processing. Then we'll turn to the page itself, with ten tips for a memo that's a model of neatness and a pleasure to read.

TO WRITE—OR TO DICTATE

Is it necessary to *write* a million-dollar memo? Can't you dictate one?

The easiest, and most popular answer would be "Of course! You've been dictating your memos for years, haven't you? Why not perfect a method you already know and like?"

But I can't go along with this answer. I must admit a prejudice. I'm partial to putting words on paper. To me, the act of writing is an act of discovery, reaching into my own knowledge and making verbal sense of it. Maybe I need the time it takes to write or type the words just to reach that knowledge. Maybe I need to *see* what I know. Speaking, for me, is too fast. When I talk about a subject, I seem to cover it all in far less time than when I write. That suggests to me that I never penetrate or explore it.

This may be a purely personal response—though I doubt it. Writing a sentence is deliberate. And the sentence stares back at you, demanding to be followed coherently and logically.

But I have another, less idiosyncratic objection to dictation. Dictation is a *public* act. If you dictate a memo to your secretary—even if you're alone with your tape recorder when you dictate—you automatically assume a self-conscious role vis-à-vis the secretary. You are "the boss." You begin to talk like a boss, or at least like a businessperson. You don't sound natural. You may sound pompous, self-important, stuffy. Just listen to yourself next time.

If you write the draft yourself, it's between you and yourself. You can dare to write freely, naturally, honestly. You can feel free to try something new—without fearing for your image.

11

In this book, you are going to learn a new way of writing. You can apply it to dictating, certainly. But you may be making it much harder for yourself by denying yourself the privacy crucial to free experimentation.

THE WORD PROCESSOR AS MEMO PRODUCER

The word processor could have been invented for the million-dollar memo. This excellent machine allows you to write as much as you like—then store the good and erase the unnecessary, all in a minimum of space and time. Its ability to remove, restore, and replace whole chunks of writing is a psychological, as well as a time-saving, aid. It has removed the onerous sense of *permanency* of the printed word.

Oh yes, that black-and-white page can be a real hurdle for the writer. I used to refuse to type drafts, even though handwriting took me much longer. Why? Because I knew I would do anything I could to avoid changing a typed manuscript. Once a page was typed—well, was I going to retype the whole thing just because one sentence looked fuzzy? Or because the tone was not quite right? I *justified* my typed pages—purely so as not to have to retype them.

But the word processor has saved us all. Its green-on-black pages are beautifully temporary. It beckons us to change, to add, subtract, make perfect. We can freely write ten pages without cease, and then pull out the best parts for the final one- or two-page memo.

SIX ADVANTAGES OF A WORD PROCESSOR

1. You can change whole passages *at the very last minute*—because you won't have to retype whole pages.

2. You can experiment with the *appearance* of your memo—trying new centering, indenting, paragraphing at will.

3. You can store all your notes *in one place* for instant, easy-to-read recall.

4. You can *shift words* . . . sentences . . . paragraphs . . . even blocks of pages . . . in seconds.

5. You can *make editorial comments* on your final copy—and simply remove them when you're ready to print.

6. You can visualize *the whole manuscript* as a single piece rather than a series of pages. You won't let the number of pages or lines on a page determine the flow of your thought. And you will have a greater feeling for the shape and organization of the whole.

If you have a word processor, use it for every part of your writing. Type in all your notes, thoughts, and other preparatory material for the memo. Get all the note cards and scraps of paper off your desk and onto the disk. You'll then be able to refer to *all* your background information at the tap of a key.

Let the word processor be your tool for all your writing and editing. As you get used to it, you will find it encourages you to explore your thoughts and gives you a quick source of references to check your accuracy. You'll write more, faster, and better.

APPEARANCE IS EVERYTHING — AT FIRST

Your reader will see your memo before he actually reads it. You can please him right from the start just by presenting it well. Here are some tips to help you produce a good-looking memo.

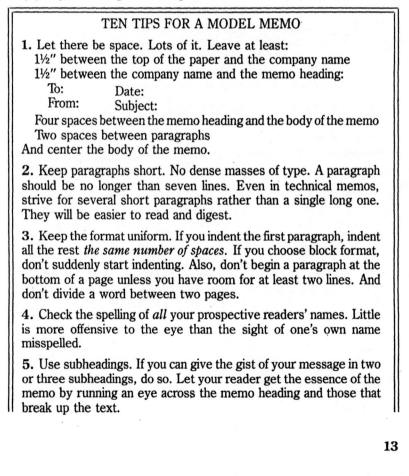

TEN TIPS FOR A MODEL MEMO

1. Let there be space. Lots of it. Leave at least:
1½" between the top of the paper and the company name
1½" between the company name and the memo heading:

To: Date:
From: Subject:

Four spaces between the memo heading and the body of the memo
Two spaces between paragraphs
And center the body of the memo.

2. Keep paragraphs short. No dense masses of type. A paragraph should be no longer than seven lines. Even in technical memos, strive for several short paragraphs rather than a single long one. They will be easier to read and digest.

3. Keep the format uniform. If you indent the first paragraph, indent all the rest *the same number of spaces*. If you choose block format, don't suddenly start indenting. Also, don't begin a paragraph at the bottom of a page unless you have room for at least two lines. And don't divide a word between two pages.

4. Check the spelling of *all* your prospective readers' names. Little is more offensive to the eye than the sight of one's own name misspelled.

5. Use subheadings. If you can give the gist of your message in two or three subheadings, do so. Let your reader get the essence of the memo by running an eye across the memo heading and those that break up the text.

13

6. No smudges. That includes dirty fingerprints, carbon paper marks, stray pencil lines, a trace of butter from your late-morning breakfast-at-the-desk. Remember, your writing reflects *you*. You wouldn't go into your boss's office with spots of tomato sauce besmirching your clothes, would you? A messy memo produces the same effect.

7. Make your signature legible. Make it large enough to express your self-confidence and clear enough to identify every letter of your name. When you sign your given name, you do so for a friendly purpose. You're saying, "Call me Ed." That purpose is *not* served if your reader can't decipher the scribble and doesn't know whether to write back to "Ted," "Ned," "Ed," or "Edie."

8. Keep to a minimum: abbreviations, punctuation marks, capitalization, and underlining. All four will mar the appearance of your typed page, if you use them to excess.

9. Write numbers as figures, not words, *except*:
  • If the number begins a sentence:
    Fifteen members of the company were there.
  • If a number from 1 to 9 occurs alone:
    Please send us four copies of the document.

10. Space properly after punctuation marks. Two spaces after the colon and all sentence enders. One space after all other punctuation marks within a sentence.

PART II

THE
$2.98 MEMO

"Then you should say what you mean," the
March Hare went on.
"I do," Alice hastily replied; "at least–at least I
mean what I say–that's the same thing, you know."
"Not the same thing a bit!" said the Hatter. "Why you
might just as well say that 'I see what I eat' is the same
thing as 'I eat what I see'!"
Lewis Carroll

Short words are best and old words when short
are best of all.
Sir Winston Churchill

4   A Typical $2.98 Memo

Here's an example of a "$2.98 memo"—the memo that's worth less than it costs to produce it. It bores, it rambles, it gets tied up in its own mouthfuls—and it does nothing for the writer. It is, unfortunately, the kind you get every day.

TO: A. M. Tyler   DATE: April 1, 1983
FROM: R. J. Smythe   SUBJECT: Training

The following is in reference to the series of training seminars which this department has been in the process of holding on varying topics on alternate Thursday evenings, generally beginning at approximately 5:30 p.m. and continuing on until 7 p.m. or in the neighborhood thereof, depending on the nature of the subject under discussion and the length of time allotted to the question period.

It has become evident that through the type of training and development program that we have been actively pursuing over the past 18 months, through the ongoing efforts of our own department and the support of other departments in the company, we have been able to make significant advances in our overall manpower level which in turn have allowed us to provide the additional technical support activities to your and other departments that I feel confident you are aware of.

In regard to the upcoming sessions in the training program, it was felt that our employees could substantially benefit from exposure to professional instruction in the areas of technical and business communication. To this intent, I made it my office to contact one R. U. Reddy, an editor and specialist in the area of technical writing. Mr. Reddy has agreed to provide us with instruction on the basic mechanics of verbal interfacing on Thursday, April 21. I, for one, expect and anticipate a stimulating and rewarding learning experience in an area unfortunately fraught with technical jargon and misunderstandings.

If you or any members of your staff would be interested in attending Mr. Reddy's session, kindly communicate same with my secretary before April 15. Seating is anticipated to be severely limited.

---

5 Business Language

On April 15, 1980, when ordinary citizens were busy preparing their tax returns, New York State Governor Hugh Carey was busy with language. He issued an executive order calling for all state agencies to rewrite their regulations in plain, understandable English. This order stated, in part:

> When pursuant to subdivision three of section two-hundred-two of the State Administrative Procedure Act an agency submits to the Secretary of State a Notice of Action Taken in which it is stated that there are substantive changes in the final action in comparison with the proposed rule or regulation, the agency shall also summarize the changes, if any, which must be made in the regulatory impact statement in order to reflect accurately the impact of the final action taken.

In other words (74 fewer): keep impact statements (whatever they are) up to date.

Heavy, bureaucratic verbiage, you sigh. But just look at the "heavies" we bring on to weigh down our language in business.

A mill manager writes that he "anticipates the possibility of requiring an additional operative" when he wants to hire someone.

A vice-president of research sends his staff a memo complaining that "there is an excessive time frame existing between your productive effort and the external communication of that effort." What he meant was "Please try to get your technical reports out faster."

WHY PEOPLE USE IT

Few of us who write like that talk like that—at least, not when we're among friends! We don't even *think* like that. No, superloquacious pomposity seems to pour mainly from the office pen. We may sit down, pen poised, thinking simply, "We must keep our program reports up to date." But bring that pen down to paper, as one executive did, and watch the fog rise:

> Prompt and effective monitoring of the program reports is an absolute necessity to assist in assessing performance data. . . .

What is happening is, literally, a translation. We translate our honest, straightforward thoughts into bumptious gobbledygook *because we think it's expected of us.* We're afraid that, if we write simply, we won't come across as important . . . impressive . . . a member in good standing of the business community. Right?

17

HOW BUSINESS LANGUAGE
HOLDS YOU BACK

We want to sound important. *Important*, in business, is practically synonymous with *large*. A large company is, by definition, important. The more important you are, the larger your paycheck, your office, your staff, your house, your expense account. So—says the aspiring manager—largeness suggests importance. If I use large words, people will consider me important. And he writes:

> This department is in a position to anticipate an immediate resumption of computational operations directly following the elimination of excess-use-related malfunctionings of the data-processing equipment.

If he hadn't needed to sound important, he would have written:

> We'll be able to get back to work as soon as they stop overloading the computer.

The trouble is—unlike large paychecks and houses and expense accounts, large *words* are not limited to important people. Just about everyone in business is using them. If you sound like everybody else, you can't expect to sound especially important.

We want to sound impressive. Business today is full of different technologies, each with its own jargon. People are running around chattering about *multiple disk drives, chemical-specific studies, discounted cash flows*—and they sound impressive. They sound like experts, especially to anyone outside their specialty. We want to sound impressive, too. So we begin spouting jargon, either managerial jargon or the techno-verbiage of our own specialty.

But again—everybody's doing it. How many experts can there be? And how impressed are *you* when someone else decides to "zero fund a program" instead of ending a project?

We want to sound like a solid member of our peer group. A teenager gasps, "And I was like: Oh no!!" A businessman declares, "My immediate reaction was, I can assure you, one of profound concern and dismay." Both mean "I was shocked." The words they chose were merely the insignia of the group with which they wish to identify.

And yes, if you earnestly want to sound like "one of the crowd" in business, you must resign yourself to a tedious, unimaginative style and vocabulary.

But people don't get promoted by being just "one of the crowd."

If you want to be crisp, clear, and a pleasure to read . . . if you want to write that million-dollar memo . . . you've got to break out of the stodgy, tongue-tied masses and let your writing flow, clearly and simply.

18

Are you wondering whether the risk might be too great? Whether, in fact, you'd do better to keep on using the accepted corporate claptrap? Then listen to Malcolm Forbes, President and Editor-in-Chief, *Forbes* Magazine:

> Be natural—write the way you talk. . . . Business jargon too often is cold, stiff, unnatural. . . . Don't put on airs. Pretense invariably impresses only the pretender.[1]

or the director of research of a large corporation:

> If you can't tell in written or oral English what your results are, it is impossible to get along in any industry. If you can't put your thoughts and figures on paper in concise, readable English—you're sunk.[2]

Convinced? Good. Then let's get rid of the excess baggage.

---

[1]Malcolm S. Forbes, "How to Write a Business Letter," *Power of the Printed Word*, International Paper Company, 1982.

[2]Quoted in Porter G. Perrin, *Writer's Guide and Index to English*, 1965.

PART III

THE ENEMIES OF A MILLION-DOLLAR MEMO

God is a verb,
not a noun.
R. Buckminster Fuller

But all the fun's in how you say a thing.
Robert Frost

6 How to Lighten Your Language

The first step in lightening your language is realizing how heavy it has become, what's making it weigh down your message. The next step is deciding to change.

That decision is not so easy. It's much easier not to change. It's safer.

Remember what I said at the beginning of Chapter 1. The key to your writing a million-dollar memo is *willingness* to try.

Are you willing to speak and write so that you will be fully understood? Do you dare give up the fuzzy phrases you once used for shelter? Are you really going to try trusting people?

These are not rhetorical questions. You must *feel* sure that you can answer "yes" before you go on. Otherwise, you'll just be shifting words around and using a few less syllables. To write a million-dollar memo, you have to think differently. Are you willing to try?

Good. Then we can look at the five "heavies" weighing down business language. You will feel your language lighten as you shed them one by one.

The five heavies are:

(1) **phony fancies**—the fake nothings you put in to sound impressive

(2) **nounery**—the overuse and piling up of nouns

(3) **the passive voice**—the confusing, deadly dull form that's the very opposite of personal communication

(4) **wasted words**—words you don't need to say what you have to say

(5) **grammar gaffes**—the mistakes that muddy your meaning

7 Forsake Phony Fancies

Phony fancies are those fuzzy words or expressions you use to sound important, impressive, or knowledgeable—often when you're feeling none of the three! They're phony because they masquerade as communication. In fact, instead of transmitting meaning, they obscure it.

After a while you'll recognize phony fancies as soon as they touch the horizon of your consciousness. You'll know them by the muddiness of their meaning, the avalanche of syllables and words, and the impossibility of your using them to talk to a friend.

Here's a basic list of phony fancies, with some clear and simple alternatives:

for the purpose of finding ...	to find ...
in reference to	about
in the amount of	for
of the order of magnitude	about
pertaining to	about
prior to	before
subsequent to	after
at such time as	when
due to the fact that	because
inasmuch as	as
in light of the fact that	since
in the event that	if
owing to the fact that	because
at an early date	soon
at the present time	now
in the majority of instances	usually
in view of the foregoing	so
be in receipt of	have

be of assistance to	help
effectuate	carry out
enclosed herewith is	enclosed is
endeavor	try
has potential for growing	may grow
initiate	begin
is of the opinion that	believes
occasion	cause
procure	get
provides for the requirements that you	enables you to
provides a means whereby you may	enables you to
take corrective action on	correct
modification	change
utilization	use

This short list is really just to give you a flavor of the phony fancies. You can make up hundreds yourself. They're probably the easiest "heavy" to create—and the easiest to avoid. You avoid them by consciously shedding your mantle of corporate self-importance (which you put on to cover up some insecurities) and determining to write as you would talk to a friend—in clear and simple English. Phony fancies simply can't live in a mind that scorns pretense or a memo that abjures pretentiousness.

8 No More Nounery

Nouns are the "solids" of language. They plant themselves firmly in sentences and phrases, and there they sit, unbudging, immovable. Some style-conscious writers have bemoaned the "noun-demons" that ruin the flow of language, but the term is not really apt. Demons move. Nouns don't.

Think about the memos, letters, or reports that you write. Most of the time, you're

- describing an event or a process
- explaining how to do something
- asking for something to be done
- putting forth a concept or theory

You're leading from one thought or action to the next. You want language that *moves,* easily and freely, to translate the flow of thought into words. Words that stop the flow of a phrase confuse or hobble the thought. The hobblers are almost always nouns.

To free your language, eliminate *nounery.* That's what I call the overuse of nouns. The main types of nounery follow.

NOUN CLUSTERS

Noun clusters are expressions, usually of three words or more, that consist entirely of nouns. The effect is literally ponderous: the reader must slow down to ponder the meaning of the expression. Take a common noun cluster, "bridge structure modifications." It contains only three words, but it's an obstruction to reading. The nouns *bridge* and *structure* have to be translated mentally into adjectives modifying "modifications." This hobbles the reading. "Changes in the structure of the bridge" may be longer, but it's much easier to read and comprehend. And effective writing is that which is easily understood—not always that which uses the fewest words.

We tend to grab hold of noun clusters when we don't want people to think we're saying what we actually *are* saying! For example:

euphemism	meaning
limited-resource-family demographic area	slums
interior intrusion detection systems	burglar alarms
cost impact consideration systems	price
schedule stretchout adjustment	delay
revenue enhancement	tax increase
employment termination	firing
profit margin reduction	loss
cost of living adjustment modifications	rising prices

And some "free gifts" from the real estate and auto industries:

handyman special	run-down house
starter home	hut
impact attenuators	bumpers

VERBS TURNED INTO NOUNS

Some expressions that start out as verbs in our heads end up as nouns on paper. For example:

he *tends*	becomes	he exhibits a *tendency* to
we should *encourage*	becomes	we should give *encourage-ment* to
I *appreciate*	becomes	allow me to express my *appreciation*
let us *consider*	becomes	let us take into *consideration*

You'll find a variation on this theme—with alternatives—on pages 111–112.

NOUNS TURNED INTO VERBS

The ultimate step in total nounery is the turning of nouns into verbs. There is no movement anymore, only static pictures. Even verbs "lose the name of action"—for they are nothing more than heavy nouns with a verbal addition:

noun	"verb"
automation	to automatize
concert	to concertize
effect	to effectuate/effectualize
finality	to finalize
impact	to impact on
interface	to interface
messenger	to messenger
priority	to prioritize
reference	to reference, to be referenced
result	to result in
solubility	to solubilize

Business writing is emblazoned with nounery. A research director may tell his assistant "Now, don't change anything here until you've checked it thoroughly." But put a piece of paper in front of him, and you're likely to get:

All aspects of the situation should be taken into careful consideration prior to the implementation of any corrective action.

WHY WE FALL VICTIM TO NOUNERY

People commit nounery in business for a couple of reasons:
 • The desire to lend weight to one's words. The research director feels that instructions concerning the "implementation of corrective action" will be taken more seriously than a request to "stop a leak." In fact, the latter is clearer and has a greater chance of being understood—and acted upon.
 • The desire to compress—to say it all in as few words as possible. We live in an age of microchips—and the effect on some of us is an obsession to cram as much as possible into the smallest imaginable space. We do this under the illusion that we are saving time. We produce outrageous mouthfuls of noun clusters to save a word or two—and achieve only confusion. "Bridge structure modifications" contains only three words, but

"changes in the structure of the bridge" is much easier to read and grasp. Remember that effective writing is that which is quickly understood—not that which uses the fewest words!

HOW TO REPLACE NOUNERY

Once you recognize the causes and symptoms of nounery, you can easily avoid it. Use *verbs* as much as possible—active, living words that tell the reader what was going on, not what "resulted." Think "flow," not "picture." And if you find a verb ending in -*ize* or a group of more than two nouns hanging around together—mistrust them. Remove them. Instead, write down what you think they mean in clear and simple English.

9 Turn the Passive Voice Around

Justly condemned as "the most deadly of business writers' paradigms," the passive voice is singularly boring, uninformative, and lifeless. It is also ubiquitous in business. Judging from most memos and reports, no recognizable individual ever *does* anything in business; activities are inscrutably performed by some unknown, or unnamed, power:

> *It is recommended that a fan pump be installed on No. 9 machine*

Who recommended it? Who will install it?

> *A wide variety of composite subjects were discussed*

By whom?

Occasionally, we do learn the identity of the agent:

> *The headbox consistency is fixed at 0.92 by drainage considerations*

Why not:

> *Drainage considerations fix the headbox consistency . . . ?*

What's wrong with the passive voice? First, it slows down the sentence with extra words. It also slows down the reader. In life, people or events *cause things to happen.* Mark sends the bill to Joe. If you write "Joe was sent the bill by Mark," the reader has to translate your sentence mentally into the logical, actual sequence: Mark sent the bill to Joe.

Furthermore, the word order of the passive voice actually reverses the logical progression of the action. Instead of *Mark (the originator)—sent—bill—Joe* we get *Joe—sent—bill—Mark.* Our minds form a mistaken image before they decode the scrambled message.

The passive voice can be terribly confusing. It engenders all sorts of misplaced modifiers. In a book on management recently submitted for publication (and returned for rewriting!), we find:

> *Assure that a program manager is established by the subcontractor with authority to speak for and commit his company . . .*

Who has the authority? The subcontractor or the program manager? The writer meant:

> *The subcontractor must appoint a program manager with authority . . .*

No confusion there.

WHY THE PASSIVE VOICE DOESN'T WORK

Remember, when you write a million-dollar memo you, personally, speak to your reader, personally. But if you write:

> Last week a directive was sent out to all members of this department . . .

the individual writer and reader disappear. Look what happens when you change it to:

> Last week I sent you a directive . . .

Both writer and reader leap back into the picture.

With all its deficiencies, why is the passive voice such a favorite with so many people in business? Look over the memos on your desk or any government reports that may have come your way. You'll have to search hard to find someone actively admitting to doing something.

And that's the reason people go passive. The passive voice is a hedge. You can hide behind it. When you say a directive was sent out, you don't have to admit to being its originator. The passive voice offers a surreptitious way to pass the buck, should you want to dissociate yourself from something you have done.

But by dissociating yourself from your actions, you also render yourself anonymous. That's not million-dollar memo style. Anonymous drudges do not shine in corporate starscapes.

Another reason many people favor the passive voice is that they believe, mistakenly, that it sounds loftier. They feel that by saying "It is believed that . . ." or "A consensus was achieved on . . ." they confer some grandeur on the people involved and on themselves as dignified writers.

They are wrong. The passive voice does not make the reader conjure up a mythical body of seers deliberating on weighty problems. It simply appears as what it is: another tedious, self-consciously pompous piece of writing. If the reader thinks highly of them and their organizations, his respect will increase on reading an active declaration of responsibility:

> *We* came to the conclusion that . . .
> *I* believe that . . .

HOW TO AVOID THE PASSIVE VOICE

Use action verbs.

Use your memos, letters, and reports to tell people what you have done. If necessary, you'll take the consequences. If something's amiss, they'll find you out anyway, passive voice or no!

If you find yourself saying such and such was done—turn the sentence around and tell who did it. Use active verbs whenever you possibly can. For more details on verbs of action, see page 136.

Talk to people. Show yourself to be definite, proud, and straightforward. Those are the qualities of the leader you want to become.

10 Weed Out Wasted Words

Wasted words are simply words that do not fill your reader's needs. They don't clarify, explain, interest, intrigue. They add nothing to your reader's pleasure or understanding. Instead, they get in the way of both.

The following words, which abound in bad business writing, have come to mean — absolutely nothing. Don't use them.

angle	— from a different *angle* = differently
area	— He is a specialist in *the area of* market research = He is a specialist in market research
aspect	— I don't feel comfortable about *the financial aspect* of the agreement = I don't think they should get half the profits
case	— *In the case of* agencies handling large volumes of letters, special provision will be made = We will make special provision for agencies handling large volumes of letters
character	— This product is of an unusually fine *character* = This product is unusually fine
circumstance	— *Circumstances* warranted a full investigation of the missing papers = Because the committee suspected fraud, we ordered a full investigation
factor	— Time was a definite *factor* in our decision = We postponed the project partly because we have so little time left this year
function	— He performed well *in his function as* interim officer = He performed well as interim officer
field	— There were several openings *in the field of* chemical engineering = There were several openings in chemical engineering
happen	— *It happened that* we were there together = We were there together
lines	— along agricultural *lines* = in agriculture

nature	— He was assertive *by nature* = He was assertive
point	— *The point is* that we are already overstaffed = We are already overstaffed
respect	— We want your advice *with respect to* possible areas of test marketing = We would like you to tell us where we should start test marketing
situation	— With respect to the current gold *situation,* we just have to sit tight = The current fluctuation in gold prices suggests that we should neither buy nor sell
thing	— We have a problem with this media *thing* = We have a problem with the media
type	— These boxes are made of a superior *type of* wood = These boxes are made of a superior wood
variety	— of a high-quality *variety* = high-quality

You can see that avoiding these words often forces you to say what you mean much more clearly. Pretty soon you'll be rejecting the nothing words before they hit paper, because you'll be demanding *work* of every word you write. No more idle words in your million-dollar prose; each must justify its existence by meaning.

Wasted words also occur, though less obviously, in *redundancies.* Redundancies are those repetitive expressions that the writer plunks into his sentences in the mistaken belief that he is intensifying the power or significance of his message. Instead, he obscures it with clutter.

Redundancies that add nothing but tedium to your tale include:

if *and only if,* then *and only then*, etc.	= if, then
each and every man and woman	= everyone
each *of these*	= each
few *in number*	= few
consensus of *opinion*	= consensus
and so *as a result*	= and so
adequate *enough*	= adequate
and moreover	= moreover
but nevertheless	= nevertheless
never *at any time*	= never

results *so far achieved*	= results
adequately satisfied	= satisfied
uniquely one of a kind	= unique *or* one of a kind
make an effort to try	= try

And courtesy of the Nixon White House:

at this point *in time*	= now
opening gambit	= gambit
draw *final* conclusions	= conclude
a hypothetical situation *that does not now exist*	= a hypothetical situation
a time of *critical* importance	= a time of importance
the *actual* tapes	= the tapes
unimpeachable integrity	= integrity

In all those expressions, the italicized words only repeated the message already in the others.

Some less striking redundancies appear in these common expressions in which the adjective duplicates a concept in the noun:

advance planning (there's no other kind of planning)

close proximity (you can't be in *far* proximity)

first priority (there's no second or third priority — despite political lingo)

And by the same reasoning:

end product	*necessary* requisite
important essentials	*new* recruits
integral part	*past* history
joint cooperation	*practical* experience
major breakthrough	*separate* entities

For a summary of types of redundancies, see page 113.

11 Clear Up Glaring Grammar Gaffes

Let's be clear about grammar. It's not a set of rules you follow because they were drummed into your head at school. I like to consider grammar *the linking of words so that they accurately transmit the writer's meaning to the reader.* Period.

What about the famous injunctions not to "split infinitives" or "end a sentence with a preposition"? These rules have a sound reason behind them. The last word of a sentence naturally receives great emphasis. If you make it a preposition, you're probably putting the emphasis on the wrong word. An infinitive is a unit—*to go; to be* or not *to be.* If you split it, you break up the unity. "I told you to go quickly" is much smoother than "I told you to quickly go." Imagine if Shakespeare had written "To be or to not be." It might still have been the question — but it wouldn't have reached the listener with such pure force.

Conversely, when split infinitives and prepositional endings are the least awkward expressions you can find—use them. Remember Churchill's retort when he was accused of that prepositional crime: "This is the sort of English up with which I will not put."

The glaring gaffes to avoid are not the school-rule breakers but the constructions that *interrupt the flow of meaning from writer to reader.*

UNCLEAR AGREEMENT

If electric ovens give better service than gas ovens, they should be replaced.

Which should be replaced? Instead, write:

If electric ovens give better service, they should replace the gas ones.

Here's another:

The accounting department informed the Dayton lab that its last figures had been off.

Whose figures? Those computed by the accounting department or those submitted by the Dayton lab? Instead, write:

The accounting department told the Dayton lab that the lab's last figures had been off.

There the agreement was unclear. Sometimes it's plain wrong.

> *A manager of great foresight, he considered her ready for a promotion.*

This sentence says *he* was a manager of great foresight. The writer didn't mean that. He should have written:

> *Considering her a manager of great foresight, he felt she was ready for a promotion.*

UNPARALLEL CONSTRUCTIONS

> *We must concentrate on the product, the publicity, the marketing opportunities and running an efficient organization.*

The unparallel gerund stops the reader in his tracks and breaks the flow of the message. Instead, write:

> *We must concentrate on the product, the publicity, and the marketing opportunities. And we must run an efficient organization.*

When you study the first sentence, you can see that *product, publicity,* and *marketing opportunities* are entities on which you can concentrate. *Running an efficient organization* is an activity you do. As it's not parallel with the other three, it demands and deserves a sentence of its own.

COMMA BLUNDERS

Only a purist will get seriously upset if you stick your comma outside, instead of within, the quotation marks. Only a few stylists will ardently dispute whether or not to place a comma before *and* in a series. Don't worry about such fripperies, unless they strike your fancy. Right now you're concerned about *transmitting the intended meaning* — and here, commas can be a help or a disaster.

A writer of a technical report began:

> *The 12-inch cleaners, which are described in this report, did not function well under stress.*

But he didn't mean it! Further reading revealed that, contrary to this statement, many of the 12-inch cleaners functioned perfectly under stress. Only certain ones failed: the ones he was about to describe. What he *meant* was:

> *The 12-inch cleaners which are described in this report did not function well under stress.*

The commas alone misrepresented the writer's meaning. When you set off a *which* or *that* clause with commas, as he did, you are saying to your reader: This clause does not change the meaning of the rest of the sentence. The rest of the sentence will make sense without it.

The reader mentally removes the comma-enclosed clause and gets, wrongly:

The 12-inch cleaners did not function well under stress.

Without the commas, however, the clause appears essential to the meaning of the rest of the sentence. You can't take it away without changing the meaning transmitted. It's all the sentence or nothing.

So—use commas to set off your *which* or *that* clauses *only* when those clauses can be removed without changing the sense of the sentence that's left.

The other frequent comma blunder that can irritate and sometimes confuse readers is the misplacement of a comma where a period belongs.

The project seemed about to be approved, it was only a matter of time.

This is just plain wrong. Commas indicate brief pauses *within* complete sentences. You can't use them to separate independent clauses. That's the period's job.

The project seemed about to be approved. It was only a matter of time.

If you want to suggest a closer connection between the two clauses, you can use a semicolon or a dash instead of a period. You'll find these punctuation marks discussed in more detail under "The Connectors," page 76.

The semicolon establishes a basic link, with no particular emphasis:

The project seemed about to be approved; it was only a matter of time.

The dash, on the other hand, sets off the second clause, calling attention to it and adding a touch of drama:

The project seemed about to be approved—it was only a matter of time.

You see how you can build drama and suspense into your memos? And are you beginning to see what fun it can all be?

Great. Now you've shaken off the worse shackles—phony fancies, nounery, the passive voice, wasted words, and grammar gaffes. Don't relax completely, though. They're still ready to tie you up again. Old habits are powerful.

Just remember that you are trying to tell someone something—clearly and simply. If you determine to do that, you won't have any room or inclination for hedging, pap, or puffery. You may still make an occasional grammatical blunder. Don't despair. Think of the German conductor Karl Richter. During a rehearsal, Richter lost his temper with an errant British trombonist. Driven beyond endurance, the conductor shouted, "Up with your damned nonsense twice or once I will put but sometimes always by God never!"

Richter's syntax could have been smarter but, according to Lord Mancroft, who tells the story, "The trombonist got the message."

PART IV

TECHNIQUES OF A MILLION-DOLLAR MEMO

*There is in writing the constant joy
of sudden discovery, of happy accident.*
H. L. Mencken

*Do you wish people to think well of you?
Don't speak well of yourself.*
Blaise Pascal

12 Phase 1: Think Like Your Reader

You've shed your shackles. Now you can get moving! The three-phase million-dollar program is clear and simple. *You can do it,* once you're rid of all that polysyllabic pap and puffery.

Think like your reader. Hardly anyone does, you know. When was the last time you sat down to write a memo and spent the first fifteen minutes trying to understand your reader? Honestly, did you ever do it? Yet we write mainly, and sometimes exclusively, to get something across to the reader—to *communicate* with him. Remember the source of that word: *communis,* common. When we write or talk, we are reaching out to touch that which is common between us and the other person. We want to make that person understand what we have to say.

When you're talking to someone, it's a lot easier. You can *see* the other person's reactions. If he hasn't understood you, you can usually tell from his face alone. And as you try to clarify yourself, you can use gestures, facial expressions, perhaps even visual aids to get your meaning across.

When you're writing, you have no way of knowing how you're being received. You have to supply the reader's reactions for yourself, in your mind's eye, using all your powers of imagination and perception. That's the best you can do.

But nobody does it! Nobody but good writers, that is. Most people rely on *language itself* as the common ground, and leave it at that. They're wrong.

LANGUAGE IS NOT A COMMON GROUND

Language as we use it isn't a common ground. We may misuse a word and confuse our readers. Or we may use the word correctly—and still confuse the readers who misunderstand it!

Take a moment to write down the meaning of the following commonly used—and more commonly abused—words. Don't look them up. Just write down what you think they mean.

biannual			predicated
climactic	fortuitous	gratuitous	prototype
enormity	fulsome	inured	transpired

39

If you thought *climactic* related to the weather, you were wrong. *Enormity* doesn't mean *hugeness* . . . *gratuitous* doesn't mean *free* . . . and no one would thank you for *fulsome* praises. That is, no one who knew what the word meant.

I'll tell you one thing about each word, though. *Chances are either you or your reader thinks it means something that it doesn't mean at all!*

═══════════Here's what the words really do mean:═══════════

biannual	.........twice a year
climactic	.........critical, acute
enormity	.........great wickedness
fortuitous	.........accidental
fulsome	.........offensive
gratuitous	.........unearned or unwarranted
inured	.........accustomed or resigned
predicated	.........affirmed, declared, based
prototype	.........original model
transpired	.........became known, came to light

If you were right on all ten words, congratulations. If not, you've learned something new. Right or wrong, you can be sure many of your readers have the wrong definition in their heads for these and other words. Yet they continue to misuse or misunderstand them without even knowing it.

The dictionaries often add to the confusion. Because so many people continue to use a word to denote something other than its original meaning, many lexicographers have felt it necessary to include this wrong usage as a fourth or fifth definition of the word. You may very well be able to cite Webster as permitting *enormity* to denote "hugeness" (fourth meaning). But — where does that permission get you? If you're using the word according to its fourth meaning, and your reader assumes you to mean the first (*wickedness*) — you might as well be writing to him in Chinese.

Stick to the first, *preferred* meaning of your words, and your meaning is more likely to coincide with your reader's understanding. Better yet — use words that no one is likely to confuse: *twice a year* instead of *biannual, offensive* instead of *fulsome,* and so on.

Language is not enough to make a common ground between writer and reader. Even words that both understand may have a different meaning for each. If I promise that "I'll send you the documents ASAP," we may both enjoy being privy to that overworked piece of business jargon. But I may mean "two weeks from tomorrow"—and you may understand "this afternoon."

Now, as you work on your million-dollar memo skills, you will find that you're writing words and expressions that your reader is very likely to understand. That's the focus of clear and simple language. But it's not enough. Remember, *communication* is not just *information*. Communication is reaching out into the common ground you share with the other person.

HOW TO GET INTO YOUR READER'S HEAD

You have to know your reader. Before you start writing, answer *all* the following questions, on paper. When it becomes a habit, you can do it in your head. If you start out doing it in your head, you'll skimp.

(1) *Who* **is going to read this?**

(2) *Why* **would he take time out to read it?**

(3) *What problems or needs* **of his does it address? Can it save him money? Bring him new, relevant knowledge? Help him in his work? Help him look better to his boss?**

(4) *How* **can it do that?**

When you answer these questions, you'll be thinking like your reader. It may seem unfair, but people don't read memos because we want them to read them or even because we feel passionately or urgently about the subject we're discussing. People read because they hope to gain something of value *to them*.

That's why you're reading this book, isn't it? Because *you* want to write better and do better—not because I want you to read it!

So, before you start writing, try to get into your reader's head. If possible, ask those questions for everyone who will read your memo. They're the basic demands we all bring to any piece of writing: *Why should I bother with this? What will it do for me? How?* If you're prepared to answer those questions, you'll have your readers *reading*. And that's already half the battle!

13 Phase 2: Write From the Right Side of Your Brain

Now that you're imbued with your reader's needs and demands, you can start to write. You're thinking like a reader, so you can be confident that you will approach your writing from the right point of view. With your answers to those questions clear in your mind, begin writing.

To remind you, the questions are: Who? Why? What? How? *Who* will read this? *Why* should he? *What problems or needs* of his does it try to answer? *How?*

And when I say begin writing, I mean just that. *Write*—with no stopping to change a word, cross out a sentence, rethink a paragraph. That's editing. It's what you do to the raw written material when it's all down. *It should not be confused with writing.*

WRITING VS. EDITING

As far as the West is from the East . . . so far should the act of Writing be from the act of Editing. They are distinct, independent activities, performed, it seems, by different halves of the brain. *Writing* is putting your thoughts into words. *Editing* is refining that verbal expression.

If you're one of those people who claim, "I hate to write," you may be doing yourself an injustice. You may think you hate to write because every time you sit down in front of a piece of paper all you end up with is a few sentences written and rewritten and rewritten. That dense scrawl is the result of trying to write and edit all at once. That's how most people approach writing. It's the way we were taught in school: correct as you go along. Nothing could be more destructive to good, flowing writing or more constipating to the writer. Your right brain forms an idea and starts to spin it out into words. Then your left brain sends out a sledgehammer to clobber a less-than-perfect word—and kills the idea with it. It's a form of self-torture.

You may never have given yourself the supreme pleasure of *just writing.* Pull out a first draft of something you wrote recently—a draft for a memo, a letter, part of a report. Do you see sentences begun, then crossed out and abandoned? Are there words written, struck through, changed—then perhaps put back all over again? Can you imagine what happened to the embryonic ideas while all this chopping and changing was going on?

HOW TO WRITE FREELY

You simply cannot *express your thoughts clearly in writing* if you're occupied in *correcting your writing* at the same time. In an excellent book on the subject, *Writing With Power,* Peter Elbow tells the writer to write his first draft for at least ten minutes without stopping—just to separate the producing from the revising process. At this stage, we should not be thinking about "how to write." Rather, we should be focusing on the subject of our discourse and allowing our creative energy to express our thoughts freely. You can see why. If you're half-focused on describing the recent activities performed by your department and half-focused on the words you're using to describe them, you will do each job half-well, at best.

HOW TO LEARN THROUGH WRITING

Also, writing has a magical power. It can actually increase your conscious knowledge! If you make yourself sit down and write all you know about a subject, with no corrections or constraints, you may well find that you know and can express a lot more than you realized. It's like sending a plumb line down to the depths of your knowledge and experience and pulling back all that's there, with no interfering signals to knock you off course. And having completed Phase 1 of the million-dollar method, you'll be writing about things that will interest your reader.

So when you sit down to write, just write. Do not allow yourself to cross out or change a single word. If you start a sentence and then feel you want to say it differently, simply go on to say it differently. No stopping sentences midway, either. Let your thoughts flow their way.

A WRITING EXERCISE

Try it. Set aside ten minutes, now. Right now. Take out a pad of paper. Sharpen a pencil or get a pen. Now pick one of the following topics:

profit

the ideal manager

business entertaining

time management at home

Write your chosen topic across the top of the first page. Then, for ten *whole* minutes, write about that topic without stopping. Make absolutely no corrections. And no fresh starts.

At the end of the ten minutes, stop writing. Put the paper away, and try to resist looking at it, preferably until tomorrow.

I think you will be surprised at the amount you have written, the logical connection of your thoughts, the thoughts themselves, and the energy of your writing.

Wait a minute. Have you done the exercise? It can't take you more than ten minutes. The rest of the book will mean more to you if you do those ten minutes of writing *now*.

Well. It wasn't easy, was it? To write purely like this is to break the habit of a lifetime. We have all been conditioned to write, cross out, and start again, hobbling along painfully to the end of our messy pages.

Why? Mainly, I think, because we're afraid of wasting time. We feel that if we can write and correct *all at once* we'll have the job done in half the time. To save the correcting for after the writing seems a crime against time!

There is only one way to overcome this fear of time-wasting. I tried it, and I have written first and edited second ever since. *Time yourself.* Make a strict account of every minute spent writing "the old way," from the moment you pull out the sheet and stare angrily at it to the moment of final typing. Then try writing "the new way." Time yourself again.

WRITING THE NEW WAY

Take out a sheet of paper and write your topic across the top of it. You might like to put your *Who? Why? What? How?* questions in pencil on the side, just to start your writing from the right point. Then look at your topic, look at your questions—and begin to write.

Write anything and everything that comes into your head on the subject, in the order it occurs to you. *Force* yourself not to alter a single word. (The effort will send you into a spin the first time, but future writing will prove it's worth it. Over the years you will save hundreds of hours.)

You will notice two things. First, after the first page or so, your speed of writing will pick up a lot—because you are gradually freeing your creative faculties of creative cramps.

Second, you'll find yourself touching on some particulars that you hadn't even considered before. Your hand will hardly be able to keep pace with your suddenly articulate thoughts. You will feel wonderfully exhilarated, for what you have just done is allow your creative forces full, free rein.

After you have written all you want to write on the subject, stop. Check to see how much time you spent on that phase of your work. Then put the writing aside and do something else. This pause is critical. It gives your critical faculties—the ones that have been resting on the left side of your brain—a chance to approach your *act of creativity* with fresh *objectivity.*

Now look at what you have written as if you were a third person examining it. You will find that you *feel* like a different person from the one who wrote the draft, for you are now the *critic,* approaching the piece from the left side of the brain. Before, you were wholly expressive. Now you are ready to edit your work.

14 Phase 3: Switch to the Left Side, and Edit

Phase 1 guided you to see the subject from your reader's point of view. Phase 2 gave you free rein to say what you wanted to say. Phase 3 is the synthesis. Now you are going to *shape* a memo that conveys the message that's important to you in a way that satisfies your readers.

SHAPING YOUR MANUSCRIPT

Editing is a much maligned word. It conjures up pictures of bespectacled drones madly slashing through manuscripts, leaving no hard-sought expression free of the scourge of their blue pencil. The new way of writing eliminates this image, because it offers an alternative. You aren't just editing in a critical or destructive way. Rather, you are shaping your spontaneous outpourings into an orderly, attractive communication. And it feels good.

Shaping is a positive, constructive act. It makes the essential difference between an unfathomable sea of thoughts and a well-charted channel between writer and reader. The blue pencil becomes an instrument of formation, not amputation.

First, I suggest that you invest in more than one colored pencil. Get yourself *five*—in different colors. Save a special one for trimming, changing, and pruning the manuscript. That will be your final task of editing. The other four—I use red, green, blue, orange, and purple all together—have different purposes.

FINDING THE UNIFYING FORCE

Your first stroke of shaping is to find the unifying force. A memo usually has a few points to make about a single subject—the subject you announce at the top of the page. In a *unified* memo, these points are connected by a single unifying force or impulse.

The *subject* of the Gettysburg Address is a memorial to the soldiers who died at the Battle of Gettysburg. The *unifying force,* the impulse behind the words that draws them all powerfully together, is Lincoln's desire *to preserve the Union.* The short address covers a great deal—the birth of the United States, its early principles, the Civil War, the battlefield, the heroic death of the men who fought there, the charge now given to the living. Yet these many points are all so strongly joined that the words seem to throb with the energy of that single impulse: *this nation must survive.* That force propels every image, as Lincoln narrows his focus from the whole country to its war, from the war to a single battlefield, from the battlefield to the men who died there—and finally, from the men who died to each single listener, the final bearer of the charge to save the country for which so many have died. The unifying force never falters.

Our regular writing tasks seldom grow from a force so powerful and urgent as this. But we always write *to say something.* If we have nothing to say, we have no reason to waste ink, paper, and a lot of people's time!

Read through your unedited draft. Then close your eyes and try to formulate a one-sentence answer to the question *What do I want to convey?* It may help to begin your answer with the words "I want." For example:

- I want you to support this new project.
- I want our company to buy the new copier I examined.
- I want better service.
- I want you to understand exactly how this machine works.

Very often you can find the unifying force only after you've written the first draft. You have to put down all your thoughts and discoveries on a subject to find out or clarify what you know and want to say about it. That is why you should write first and shape later. You'll find you have something ·real to shape!

When you've discerned the unifying force in your writing, you'll be able to extract the points you've made in its service. Underline in one of your four non-editing colors—I use purple—every sentence that carries this force through the draft. These sentences may:

(1) state a relevant point

(2) illustrate or explain a point already made

(3) connect one point or thought to another

MEETING YOUR READER'S NEEDS

Your purple lines will show you the spine of your memo. Now take your other colors and use them to underline sentences that answer your reader's three questions: Why should I read this? What needs of mine will it answer? How? Use a different color for each question.

Now—look at your multicolored memo. It should be a picture in four colors. If one color is missing, it means you haven't answered a reader's question. Find a place to do so. You might have three different colored lines under a single sentence or paragraph. That's fine—so long as that material winds up at the beginning. But one paragraph devoted to only one question is almost never enough.

Arrange your rough draft so that it follows the shape of your reader's interest. You can go back to the dialogue method given in Chapter 2. Sometimes you'll find the shape is already there, since Phase 1 had you thinking in the right direction.

The ideal "look" of your final, unscrambled draft is an unbroken purple line with green, blue, and orange appearing one after the other.

As you become more proficient in this technique, you may decide to put away your palette and just work with the purple pencil, for the spine, and the red one for final trimming. But don't toss the others out. They will save many a future memo or report that threatens to get out of hand.

EFFECTIVE ENDINGS

Before you put your pencils aside, think about the ending of your memo. It will stay with your reader. It's your last chance to make him feel like doing what you want done. It's important.

Don't just restate everything you've said in a one-paragraph wrap-up. Such a monstrosity usually serves only to destroy the clarity and simplicity of your memo.

Instead, decide to give the reader *one* item to remember. Just one. Then you can be sure he will remember it.

You may want to emphasize a point that will convince your reader to do as you wish.

> *Buying this machine now may well save us several thousands of dollars over the next five years.*

Or you may want to make your ending a signpost that guides your reader to the step following this memo:

> *Thank you for considering this proposal. I look forward to discussing it with you in detail at our meeting on Monday, March 1.*

I do not advocate leaving any critical information for the last paragraph. Your reader will wonder, with justifiable irritation, why you didn't tell him such important news at the beginning. He'll resent you for stringing him along. *But*—you can sometimes end your memo on an interesting, provocative note. For instance:

> *This series has attracted more than 450 members of the company so far. Come to the opening lecture, Tuesday, May 7, if only to see what persuaded them all to take a later train home—five nights in a row.*

When you're shaping your memo, look for any little points of interest that could be left to the last paragraph—such as the note that 450 people have already attended this series of lectures. It's always effective to end your memo with a bang, not a whimper. But don't push it. If nothing suggests itself as a punch line, don't try to manufacture one. Don't try to be clever, witty, or astonishing. If you do, you will sound as if you are *trying* to be clever, witty, and astonishing. And you will end up appearing simply silly.

So — when planning your ending, keep in mind three points:

(1) Show goodwill — that's what the reader will take away with him.

(2) Tell the reader one important item.

(3) Either remind him of *what he should know* from reading this memo or *what he should do as a result of it.*

MAKING YOUR MEMO GOOD TO READ — TWO CHECKLISTS

Now that you have a form for your memo, give it the final touch. Make it good to read. Here's the moment for that special color pencil, which you can use by following a checklist.

Trim away:

• *Clichés.* Expressions such as "last but not least," "in the final analysis," "in actual fact," and "back to square one" are unoriginal phrases that have lost their precision through overuse. Now they only cover up the writer's personality, because they're used by everybody, with the same stultifying effect. You'll find a list of some of the worst on page 140. Avoid them.

• *Irrelevant detail* that draws attention away from the unifying force.

• *Excessive explanation of the obvious.* Watch out for sentences beginning with "That is to say . . . " or "In other words . . . " If you've said it clearly, you don't always *need* to say it in other words.

• Unnecessary modifiers, such as "a *loud* explosion," "a *high* peak," "an *empty* vacuum," or "the *most* unique product."

Check for:

• *Agreement of subject and verb:* "The data *prove* (not *proves*) that . . . " (*Data* is a plural noun.) "The list of the members who are attending the lectures *is* (not are) . . . " (The subject of the verb is *list.*)

• *Correct punctuation,* particularly commas that may change meaning: "Next, we prepared the steaks in the freezer . . . " *not* "Next, we prepared the steaks, in the freezer . . . " (Unless you mean you worked in subzero temperatures.)

• *Variety* in words, expressions, and the structure and length of sentences.

• *Relationships.* Are your ideas clearly connected? Could you show the relationships better by using conjunctions (such as *because, since, yet*) instead of writing two independent sentences? Instead of: *The speaker used many visual aids. His experiment was made clear to all of us* ... try: *Because the speaker used many visual aids, we all understood his experiment.* (You got rid of the passive voice, too!)

• *Completeness.* Have you said what you promised to say?

• *Coherence.* Does your memo have a beginning, a middle, and an end? And are they connected?

Now time yourself. How long did you spend on that memo, from the first moment of writing to the last stroke of the editing pencil? Much more important: Are you pleased with the results?

Aside from anything else, this way of writing and editing is fun! It's fulfilling, because you give your creativity total freedom and your critical faculties total power. You can only do both if you write first and edit later.

To be sure of getting the best from both sides of your brain, you should allot equal time to each. Allow yourself a certain period for writing your memo—and be realistic. If you've got only an hour to spare, give it an hour. Give yourself a minimum of five minutes for Phase 1. Divide the remaining time between Phases 2 and 3, say, 25 minutes to write and 25 minutes to edit. You may even have five minutes left to tinker with your finished work. But don't skimp on the editing time. Once you start that wonderful, free-flowing writing, you won't want to stop. That's great. But you have to, if you want a good memo.

Editing, or shaping, requires time and discipline. Are you willing to give it what it needs? The reward is clear: you will be read. With pleasure.

15 Tone — Your Attitude, in Writing

The *tone* of your writing is the verbal rendition of your attitude toward your reader. It's the written translation of a smile, a scowl, a haughtily raised eyebrow, or a subserviently bowed head. The tone you use affects your readers every bit as much as the actual words, for it is in itself a message. The tone may convey attitudes you never intended to let show, such as "I'm groveling at your feet," "I'm more intelligent than you are," "You may be my boss, but you're too dumb to understand technical data," "I know what you need better than you do"—or just about anything else that we don't actually put into words. It can make or break your memo.

HOW TO IDENTIFY THE TONE OF YOUR MEMOS

The first step to controlling your tone is to be aware of it. Take a moment to go through copies of some recent memos you've written to different people. Imagine they were written by someone else, and then describe that person's relationship to the recipient of the memo. Was it: a friend trying to sound like a business associate? a business associate trying to sound like a friend? an angry customer? a willing subordinate? a friendly colleague? When you've identified the relationship, you've identified the tone, for the tone is the expression of that assumed relationship.

Now that you recognize the tone, look at the memos again. This time, imagine that you are the recipient. How do you react to the tone the writer adopted? Do you find it pompous? degrading? overly subservient? Above all, does this piece of writing make you sympathetic to the writer and willing to comply with his wishes?

You see, when you assume a role, and consequently a tone, you are by extension assuming a role for your readers. If you're the controller, they're the puppets. If you're the smart guy, they're the dumbos.

HOW TO CONTROL YOUR TONE

The wrong tone can hopelessly complicate your message. Yet the solution is so simple. There is really only one tone to adopt for everything you write to anyone in the world. That tone is *respect*. Not fear, not adoration, not subservience. Just respect.

What if you don't respect your reader? What if you consider him just an opportunistic, mindless player of office politics? All I can tell you is, if that's what you think of him, that's the message that he will receive. And it will not predispose him to grant you a raise.

Before you write, try to find something in your reader that you can sincerely respect. If you can't find a single quality, determine to respect him as another human being. Speak to the quality of the side of the person that you do respect.

Recently, I received an invitation to join a professional society. The words expressed interest in me, a sense of conviction that I would add to the quality of the society, and more of the same. On the surface, or judging from the words alone, I should have been at least flattered. Instead, I was irritated. Why? I reread the silky, creamy prose. And I realized that, although the words flattered, the tone insulted. Beneath the words, the writer was saying, "I just know I can get you to fork up $35 if I flatter you and make you think *we* think you're important!" Despite his panegyric, the writer had assumed a role of scornful superiority to me, the poor fool who would be taken in by all this insincere praise. I threw the "invitation" away without even looking into the society itself.

If that writer had adopted an attitude of respect toward his unknown readers, he would have written a different invitation. Instead of dwelling on our marvelous qualities, he would have told us what advantages he thought we would enjoy through membership in the society. If you really respect someone, you don't keep telling him so! Remember Mark Antony's damning repetition, "And Brutus is an *honorable man*."

Try to respect your reader honestly, and he will respect you. If you can't respect him, at least treat him as a human being equal to *you*. Remember, your attitude will largely determine his response.

16 Style–<u>You</u> in Your Writing

Style is not a garnish. Style is *you* in your writing. As you grow more comfortable with writing, you will enjoy watching your own personal style evolve. Style is the personality that breathes through the written words. It's the life, if you like, of the written word.

It's what is conspicuously absent from most business writing—and its absence is nothing less than the absence of life. Look at this business letter:

> As per our conversation on May 24, enclosed please find a copy of the document in question. It would be appreciated if copies of the patent could be made available as soon as possible in order for a determination to be made as to whether the present outside efforts in this area fall under the umbrella of the aforesaid patent.

The writer of that letter is actually a gregarious person and has a lively personality. Where is it, in his writing? Where is *any* personality in that piece of "communication"? There is none. The writer divested himself of his own personality when he sat down and drew on the heavy role of *businessperson.* He ground out the words that he deemed appropriate for that amorphous creature in a pinstriped suit. He disappeared, taking all his personal style with him. The result, as you can see, is deadly.

Style is personal, and, as I said, only you can find your own. But an attractive style must grow out of strong, lithe technique. That technique is *clear and simple writing.* If you work to trim all the fat and falsity from your writing, you *will* achieve a vivid, engaging, surprisingly individual style.

FIVE TECHNIQUES FOR LETTING YOUR STYLE SHINE THROUGH

Here are five rules to give you a clear and simple way of writing that will allow your own style to breathe through:

1. *Write only one thought in a sentence.* Allowing just one thought to a sentence keeps your sentences reasonably short. This single criterion will rid your writing of all sorts of muddling complexities. Look at this disaster:

> *Furthermore, since it is generally true that the longer a program is extended, the higher the costs will be, it is incumbent upon the administration to keep to a minimum any potential delays.*

53

Whew! Let's make it clear and simple, with one thought to a sentence:

If you extend a program, your costs will probably rise. Therefore, the administration should work hard to avoid all possible delays.

2. Use personal pronouns (I, you, we, they). *Talk* to your reader. Instead of announcing "The effects of this change *can be seen* in . . ." write *"You can see* the effects of this change in . . ." Then your reader is much more likely to see them! Instead of *"It should be recognized* that . . ." try "I noted that . . ." Replace "The *x is utilized* for . . ." with *"We use* the *x* for . . ." When you eschew the passive voice and put people back into the picture, the picture comes back to life.

3. *Write positively, not negatively.* To avoid committing themselves, many business writers resort to the double negative. It's confusing and unnecessary. "The profits were *not less than 50 per cent in excess of* projected figures" is a mind-muddying mouthful. What the writer means is "The profits were *at least 50 percent higher* than projected."

4. *Write about people, not dehumanized abstractions.* It is so simple and accurate to write "Twelve people will be working on the project. These include . . ." Yet a proposal I recently read said, "The total manpower required for the project is twelve agents broken down as follows." Generally, as we read, we try to translate the words into images for ourselves. The more clearly we can do this, the more effective the communication. I can see "twelve people"—but I can't visualize "manpower." And "twelve agents broken down" makes me imagine some natural disaster.

5. *Write in English.* Not in jargon. "FYI. Pls RSVP ASAP" is only a slight exaggeration of the type of "communication" going on in business. Jargon is not only dull and irritating; it's usually unclear. If you write "Please advise us on the foregoing," do you mean you want advice? or a decision? on *everything* you have written up to that sentence? or what??? If you write your request in clear and simple English, your reader will understand you and thank you for saving him the trouble of translation. "Please let us know if you accept this agreement. If not, kindly indicate the changes you wish us to make." That's clear, simple, courteous English.

17 Punctuation—The Voice Behind the Writing

It's not a matter of dots and dashes, you know. Punctuation is the staff of writing, the power we pack behind the words we choose to communicate our meaning. It's what makes a sentence stand up, bend over, lean back, or march straight out at you. Used correctly, it prevents unintentional ambiguities. Sprinkled thoughtlessly about, it can actually distort the sense of the sentence, conveying something entirely different from what you wanted to say.

What *is* punctuation? It is literally the written translation of the inflection of speech: the pauses, the emphases, the raised or lowered pitch you use to invest words with your own intent. It separates ideas, clarifies the logic of your expression, and gives your writing dynamics.

How important is it? Well, you saw the disastrous effects of comma blunders, in Chapter 11. Now let's look at *that* sentence without punctuation.

COMMAS

Well you saw the disastrous effects of comma blunders in Chapter 11. Minus the commas, the sentence says: The comma blunders made in Chapter 11 showed you well what disastrous effects they can have. And that is certainly *not* what I intended to say!

Okay. Correct punctuation is *essential* to effective communication. Since the comma, as the most frequently employed, is still the worst troublemaker, let's review the rules that will put you in control of it.

• Use commas to set off a subordinate clause *only* if the main clause could stand alone, unchanged, without it.

> *The technician, who works for Doyt Enterprises, quickly explained the problem.*

This sentence says: The technician quickly explained the problem. He works for Doyt Enterprises.

> *The technician who works for Doyt Enterprises quickly explained the problem.*

This sentence says: *The particular technician who works for Doyt Enterprises* explained the problem. It implies that there were other technicians present, none of whom exhibited the expertise of the Doyt Enterprises man.

- Use commas to separate two or more adjectives *only* if the noun could stand alone, unchanged, without any of them.

He is a brilliant, hardworking engineer.

This sentence can be divided into: He is an engineer. He is brilliant and hardworking.

He is a brilliant chemical engineer.

Now try to separate the sentence. You get: He is an engineer. He is brilliant and chemical. No good! *Chemical* changes the meaning of *engineer.* It merges with it to make a new concept. The noun *engineer* cannot stand alone without the adjective *chemical* without changing its meaning. So— use no comma.

If you're ever in doubt whether "to comma or not to comma," just take the adjectives away and see what you have left. Then try to put the adjectives alone in another sentence (*He is* . . .). If the noun now means something different and if the adjectives don't make much sense by themselves, you don't need a comma.

You can see from these two rules that the comma is an instrument of *separation* as much as an indication of a pause. A phrase or a sentence whose every word is essential requires no commas.

> Commas give you another test for your writing. If your page is filled with them, perhaps you're pouring on a little too much gravy!

THE ENCLOSERS

The comma is a small separator. Now let's look at the *enclosers*—brackets, parentheses, and quotation marks.

Brackets

Brackets [ ] are a pretty rare species. They rarely venture outside technical papers, where they serve to enclose references and perform a few more arcane functions. When they do find their way into nontechnical writing, brackets are usually used for enclosures within parentheses. In this function, they add more information to a sentence but badly break up its coherence and flow.

56

Parentheses

Parentheses ( ) enclose

The procedure followed (one developed for the F-19 project but adapted to fit present purposes) showed a great variance in molecular distribution [Fig. 23].

So far, so good. Now here's the overriding rule for brackets and parentheses: They intrude. Avoid them.

Too often, we start writing about a subject but get suddenly waylaid by a tangential idea that rushes in to be included. What do we do? Stick it in parentheses! This is fine for Phase 2 free-flowing writing, but not for the final copy. The parentheses reflect uncontrolled, unfocused thought. They *deflect* attention from the main message.

In the example I gave, the writer's main message is: The procedure showed a great variance in molecular distribution. But the sentence contains two other messages as well. One, the procedure was developed for another project and adapted for this one. Two, the reader should search for Figure 23. The two enclosers are too distracting. They stop the flow of reading.

An occasional bracketed reference is all right, though I still prefer to keep one thought to a sentence. I would add a sentence saying simply: See Figure 23. But a page full of references is barely readable. It suggests that the reader should keep flipping wildly from sentence to figure to sentence to table. . . . If you have to make many references to supporting material, use footnotes. Then your reader can choose when to look at the figure, instead of having his reading disturbed by repeated instructions to do so.

When you start to write a parenthetical expression in your final copy, stop. See if you can make that expression:

• part of the sentence, clearly related to its message

• another complete sentence

• a footnote.

If none of these fit, ask yourself why you need the expression at all.

If you *must* use parentheses, keep the enclosed material short. And remember that punctuation marks go *outside* the parentheses if they refer to the sentence as a whole, *inside* if they belong to the parenthetical expression. For example:

The mayor (who was wearing a white hat with a red peacock feather in it!) stumbled as he stepped up to the dais.

I rushed up to speak to the mayor (who seemed on the point of leaving).

I rushed up to the mayor when he was on the point of leaving. (He was still wearing the peacock feather.)

Quotation marks

Quotation marks offer an opportunity to inject a new voice into your writing, giving it more variety and verve. Feel the difference between the direct quotation:

> *The president said, "Let's get some more men on our team!"*
> and the lackluster indirect form:
> *The president said that we needed more men on the team.*

Quotation marks are used to enclose all quoted words as well as unusual terms:

> *He persisted in calling the electronic switches "doohickies."*

But — you can't make an ordinary word extraordinary by putting quotation marks around it! For instance:

The policy we are advocating can hardly be considered *"extreme."*
The quotation marks add nothing to this statement. They form merely an irritating, unnecessary addition, stuck in because the writer wanted to make an everyday word stand out. They do not work any magic on *extreme.*

If the writer wants to get special attention, *he has to say something attention-getting:*

> *The policy we are advocating can hardly be considered extreme. If it isn't followed, this agency will probably lose its two major accounts.*

No need for false quotation marks here — the facts are enough.

Punctuation with quotation marks defies logic. It is perfectly sensible for all punctuation marks but the comma and period. All other marks — exclamation mark, question mark, and all the rest—go *inside* the quotation marks if they refer to the quotation, *outside* if they belong to the surrounding sentence.

> *Did Einstein actually say it was "all relative"? No, but Archimedes was heard to shout "Eureka!"*

That part makes sense. But, curiously, the period and comma *always* go inside the quotation marks, whether or not they refer to the quotation itself or to the sentence as a whole.

> *Einstein didn't actually say it was "all relative."*

THE CONNECTORS

There's one more group of punctuation marks to master: the connectors. This includes the semicolon, the dash, the colon, the apostrophe, and the hyphen.

The semicolon and dash

The semicolon and the dash are alternatives to the period, used to indicate a close relationship between two independent clauses. The semicolon merely establishes that relationship. The dash is an attention-grabber, a rein-puller, an imperious gesture that points dramatically to the idea to follow.

Each sample shows complete fiber content—a guarantee of superiority.

Remember that *dash* rhymes with *panache*, and you'll know when to use it.

The colon

The colon is simply an arrow. It points unemotionally to information that proves, details, or fulfills the statement made. Use it before lists, definitions, and long quotations. Any time you want to translate the words "the following" into a punctuation mark, use the colon.

The memo should have three parts: a beginning, a middle, and an end.

The apostrophe

The apostrophe can tighten your discourse by its quick expression of possession. *The managers' reports* reads better than the mouthful *the reports of the managers.* Just remember to place the apostrophe *outside* plural forms to distinguish them from the singular. *The manager's reports* belong to only one manager. And if you've got a compound expression, the apostrophe follows the last part only: *the managers and directors' lunch.*

The hyphen

The only problem with the hyphen is when to use it. If you're not sure, and the dictionary doesn't help, ask yourself one question: Would the expression be confusing or difficult to read without the hyphen? If so, use it. Here are some examples of confusion that the hyphen makes plain:

chemical containing polymers

chemical-containing polymers

a light weight lifter

a light-weight lifter

coopt

co-opt

recover (from an illness)

re-cover (a sofa)

Good writing creates coherent, logical patterns and conclusions out of a barrage of thoughts. Enclosers can interrupt this process, translating instead the randomness of thought into confusing messages. Connectors can do the opposite by establishing relationships between thoughts.

18 Spelling—Write It Right

Spelling bees may be part of your past—but misspelled words can annoy your reader as much as they did that third-grade teacher of long ago. Recently, I read a paper whose writer kept hoping he wouldn't "embarass" his colleagues. While he kept hoping, *I* kept waiting for that word to recur, and every time it did, my irritation with the writer increased. His simple misspelling deflected my attention from his message.

Misspellings can harm your memo. They bother the reader; they call attention to themselves; and they make *you* look either careless or ignorant. A bit of attention to the number of *r*'s and *s*'s and the order of *i* and *e* can do wonders for your image.

=====Here's a list of words whose spelling bothers all of us: =====

accommodate	—double *c* and double *m*
battalion	—two *t*'s one *l*
characteristic	—first *a*, then *e*
commemorate	—two *m*'s, then one
committee	—double *m*, double *t*, double *e*
embarrass	—double *r* and double *s*
exaggerate	—two *g*'s, one *r*
fulfillment	—one *l*, then two
harass	—one *r*, two *s*'s
judgment	—no *e* after the *g*

liaison	—two *i*'s around the *a*
liquefy	—with an *e*
minuscule	—with a *u*
occurred	—two *c*'s, two *r*'s
pavilion	—all single letters
prevalent	—*a*, then *e*
privilege	—*i*, then *e*
recommend	—one *c*, two *m*'s
seize	—*e* before *i* (remember: you have to *see* to seize)
siege	—*i* before *e* (don't mix it up with *seize*)
separate	—two *a*'s
sincerely	—two *e*'s
supersede	—all *s*'s, no *c*'s
vilify	—one *l*
weird	—*e* before *i*

This list contains the most troublesome words you have to use. Keep it available for easy consultation. And never sit down to write anything without a dictionary handy. If in doubt, check. Having your memo proofread by a second or third party doesn't hurt either.

19 Prepositions — Little Words Mean a Lot

Small as they are, prepositions can change the meaning of your sentence and transmit something you had no desire to say.

Consider the prepositions following *adapt*. "Adapt *for*" means "prepare for a specific purpose."

> The novel was *adapted for* the stage.

"Adapt *from*" means "take or abstract from something else."

> The painting was *adapted from* a photograph.

"Adapt *to*" means "adjust to fit certain conditions."

> The species was able to *adapt* itself *to* the new climate.

Or look at "concerned *about*" vs. "concerned *in*." If you're *concerned about* a strike, you're worried about it. If you're *concerned in* it, you're out on the picket lines.

Little words can mean a lot. If you use the wrong one, you can throw your readers off balance, or at least annoy them. Either way, you'll damage your communication.

Remember which prepositions to use, and you won't have to waste any more time or energy worrying about irritating little *at*s, *to*s, or *for*s!

PREPOSITION COMBOS THAT CAUSE CONFUSION

The following list gives you the preposition combos that are most likely to trouble you. Keep it handy with your spelling list—and never be embarrassed to refer to it, even for the thousandth time.

---

admit *to*   = to confess
Jones *admitted to* falsifying the documents.
admit *into*   = to allow entry
My colleague had us *admitted into* the club.

agree *to*   = to give assent
The director *agreed to* the change in schedule.

---

agree *with* = to be of the same opinion
I agree *with you* on all your conclusions.

agree *on* = to be in accord with someone
At last we *agreed on* a conference site for next year.

compare *to* = to point out likenesses
The consultant *compared* our methods *to* those he had recently observed in Japan.

compare *with* = to point out differences
This department shows a low productivity, *compared with* the output of the other research labs.

correspond *to* = to fit, match
The dimensions of the model do not *correspond to* those of the actual machine.

correspond *with* = to exchange letters
This client *corresponds with* us quite regularly.

differ *from* = to be different from
He *differs from* me in personality, not in beliefs.

differ *with* = to disagree with a person

differ *on* = to have opposing ideas on a problem
I agree with your diagnosis. But I *differ with* you *on* the treatment you propose.

impatient *at* = refers to behavior
I was *impatient at* his inability to come to the point.

impatient with = refers to a person
Don't be *impatient with* trainees. They are here to learn.

in behalf of = in someone's interest
I felt I had to speak up *in his behalf.*

on behalf of = representing someone.
I am appearing *on behalf of* Dr. Wallace.

WORDS THAT TAKE ONLY ONE PREPOSITION

The next list is easier. These are words that accept only one preposition in preferred usage — though often not the preposition we try to hang on to them.

ability *to* (not *of*)
You have the *ability to* do far more than this job allows.

according *to* (not *with*)
According to Mr. Simmons, the profit picture looks brighter.

acquiesce *in* (not *to*)
The committee quickly *acquiesced in* the chairman's proposal.

apropos *of* (always followed by *of*)
Apropos of your suggestion, we plan to start the meeting at nine.

authority *on* (not *about*)
He is a world *authority on* solar energy.

comply *with* (not *to*)
If they do not *comply with* the new regulations, their goods will not be sold.

different *from* (not *than*)
The present departmental requirements are *different from* those of previous years.

forbid *to* (not *from*)
He told us to *forbid* them *to* leave before the session was over.

prohibit *from* (not *to*)
He told us to *prohibit* them *from* leaving before the session was over.

identical *with* (not *to*)
These samples are *identical with* the ones you sent us last year.

oblivious *of* (not *to*)
The president's mother was clearly *oblivious of* the sensation caused by her remarks.

Finally, you can't get rid of a preposition. If you use two words that require different prepositions, you have to use *both* prepositions.

The visual aids increased our interest *in* and attention *to* the lecture.
(*Not* . . . our interest and attention to the lecture.)

65

I find this repeated appearance of little prepositions irritating. The prepositions interrupt the flow of thought. I prefer a longer version that doesn't require two prepositional interruptions:

> The visual aids made us pay more attention to the lecture and increased our interest in it.*

If you have two words that both take the same preposition, you're in luck. You need to use that preposition only after the last word:

> He felt he could comply, though not agree, with their demands.

And that's probably just how you feel about prepositions!

---

*For another way to keep prepositions in their place, see page 112.

20 Metaphors — Don't Mix Them

Like most misspelled words and misused prepositions, mixed metaphors generally annoy rather than confuse readers. But irritation saps the million-dollar effect right out of your memo.

When you conclude a pep-up memo to your staff with the words "Let's all keep our nose to the wheel and our shoulder to the grindstone," no one is likely to misunderstand you. But you may get some discreet snickers.

Most common metaphors are now nothing but clichés. Indeed, most clichés began as highly original metaphors. Because they were so startlingly effective, people snatched them up and sprinkled them into their speech and writing at every possible opportunity. In so doing, they robbed the metaphors of their original freshness, their specificity, and their surprise. The metaphors became—clichés.

Hamlet speaks of the disastrous mission of Rosencrantz and Guildenstern to England, where their treachery to him will turn against them and cause their own deaths. As he contemplates this result, Hamlet muses:

> For 'tis the sport to have the engineer
> *Hoist with his own petar.*

He means, literally, "blown up (*hoist*) with his own explosive device (*petar*)." The expression is apt, vivid, and new in Shakespeare's play. But I have heard it used again and again by people who think *hoist*, here, has the modern meaning of "raise," and who therefore assume that a *petard* (the modern spelling) must be something with which you raise something else! Used today, the expression lacks not only its original freshness and topicality but also its very meaning. It has come to mean—nothing.

Most of the "metaphors" we use today have absolutely no meaning for us. Who of your colleagues has ever even seen a grindstone? Have you? When you use the expression, do you really mean to evoke the image of men toiling round a heavy millstone (grindstone), leaning their shoulders in toward the stone as they turn it to grind grain? That is the scene to which the expression refers. But we, today, have held on to these once-colorful expressions drawn from the world of pre-industrial physical labor—without having a notion of what they mean. If we *saw* the image, we couldn't possibly mix the metaphor. We don't see it. Too lazy to think for ourselves, we merely reach for the nearest cliché. Then, wanting to impart

67

a feeling of urgency, we add another cliché for good measure. And we get a mixed metaphor.

You won't mix up wheels and grindstones if you determine *never to use an expression that you don't understand.* If you aren't sure of the actual meaning of a phrase, don't use it. Or find out.

Better yet—*far* better yet—avoid all metaphors that you haven't created yourself. If you haven't thought of it, chances are it's an overused, abused, impotent cliché. It inflates your message. It does nothing useful. If you bungle it, it may even make you look ridiculous.

These mixed or senseless expressions all appeared in business letters. If the writers had understood the meaning of the words or expressions they were using, they could never have made these ludicrous mistakes:

> It's a *mute* point. (A point with its larynx removed?)
> He *threw a cold shoulder* on that *kettle of fish.* (A cannibal's bouillabaisse?)
> You must get them to *tow* the line. (To a place where the lines are allowed to park?)

And in a *Washington Post* article quoting Edward E. David, Jr., President Nixon's last science adviser:

> The White House advisers to Mr. Nixon thought that the scientists were using science as a sledgehammer to grind their political axes.

21 The Follow-up — The Final Flourish

Even the most effective memo may need to be followed up some time later. Especially if you're requesting something that the reader would prefer to postpone. A small, friendly reminder won't annoy anyone—provided it *is* small and friendly! And it can make the difference between a quick and a delayed response.

How you choose to follow up your memo depends on you, your reader, and the memo. You may write a note. You may make a phone call. You might even find a perfectly apt cartoon to send. If you sent a memo to an office out of town and you absolutely want to be noticed—you can send a telegram.

Whatever vehicle you prefer, remember that you are sending a follow-up to your memo—not an accusation. If you wait too long to send it, your reader will take it as a note of reproach for his not having responded immediately. If this is what you want to send — skip to the chapter on complaint letters (pages 99 to 108). Your note does not constitute a follow-up.

A follow-up is simply a little tap on the shoulder, with a wink and a grin. You should send it *before* the reader has had much time to act. Of course, if he acts immediately, you won't have to worry about following up!

The first requirement of a good follow-up is that it be *short*. If you've written a good memo, you haven't a lot to add. And no reader will appreciate two memos on one subject.

The second requirement is that it be *courteous*. A follow-up is a delicate piece of work. You will certainly offend the reader if you just "sling a brick" at him to remind him of what you want! Your note may consist of only two sentences — but let the first one be a humorous, gracious, or appreciative remark. Don't remind him until you have *filled a need*.

If you do not know your reader well or if you are on fairly formal terms with him, a simple, straightforward note is usually the best form of follow-up. A phone call may appear obtrusive, a cartoon inappropriate, and a telegram just too much. Just write him a note telling him you were glad to have the chance to air your ideas or tell him of your plans, and that you look forward to working with him on them. Leave it at that. Don't be smarmy or ingratiating. And don't fill more than a quarter of a page.

If you do know your reader, you have more freedom to expand your imaginative powers. I have a friend who studies *New Yorker* cartoons with

Holmesian deliberation, always searching for ones that "might come in handy one day." He has a file of them, and he almost always has just the right one to send to remind someone to do something! The recipient gets a laugh as well as a reminder, and everyone is in a good mood to get on with the job. Why not start such a file yourself?

You can do the same with newspaper or trade magazine articles. Before you write your memo, you might casually scan your literature to see if there's an appropriate clipping on the subject. Cut it out and save it for a follow-up. You need only add a line remarking on its aptness and the clear importance of the subject.

If you plan on making a phone call, try to find something new to say about the subject of the memo—or about anything else. People don't take too kindly to a peremptory ding-a-ling just to remind them that they've got a job to do. As with all your other communications, give your reader something to satisfy him first—here, a piece of information that he needs or will find interesting. Then your reminder will reach receptive ears.

If you choose a telegram for its particular dramatic flair, *really* make it short. No one ignores a telegram, so you won't have to compete for your reader's attention. Just be superfriendly and superquick! LATEST LAB REPORTS ON THE EXUTRIM PROJECT EXCITING. LOOK FORWARD TO WORKING WITH YOU ON IT. If you don't have anything new to report—don't send a telegram. Telegrams suggest news of urgency and importance. The reader's anticipation will be most unrewarded if, having ripped open his telegram, he finds merely: LOOKING FORWARD TO WORKING WITH YOU ON EXUTRIM. He'll feel cheated. And a little foolish for expecting something more exciting. No, save your telegrams for the occasions when you have something new and interesting to say — or to hint.

When should you send a follow-up to your memo or letter? Very simply: when you are sure that your message or request warrants another ten minutes of your reader's busy life. But make certain he gets some pleasure out of those extra ten minutes you're appropriating. Remember, your follow-up is meant to be a tap on the shoulder, not a jab in the ribs. And that tap should induce a smile, as well as a nod.

And that's it! Now you're all set to produce a million-dollar memo, letter, or report. Let's have one more look at the principles of a million-dollar memo.

Then pick them up and put them to work for the *immediate* betterment of your working life and your rising career.

PART V

OTHER APPLICATIONS OF YOUR MILLION-DOLLAR MEMO SKILLS

*Life is not so short but that there is
always time for courtesy.*
Ralph Waldo Emerson

*Whatever kind of word thou speakest,
the like shalt thou hear.*
Anonymous

22 How to Write a Nicely Spoken Letter

Like the secret of the million-dollar memo, the art of the nicely spoken letter is clear and simple. You begin graciously with a sincere statement of goodwill. You then go straight to the point, making your request or giving the information sought. Whenever possible, stress the positive. And you close with a specific remark, either thanking the reader for something or giving him a gentle reminder.

But most letters are doomed to bore from the start, because of their bad beginnings. Here's a list of them.

BAD BEGINNINGS . . .	AND GOOD ONES
Pursuant to your request, we enclose herewith the copy of . . .	I am happy to enclose your copy of . . .
Further to our telephone conversation this morning, I take pleasure in forwarding . . .	Here is the . . . that I promised you this morning
As per your request, enclosed please find . . .	The . . . you asked for is enclosed
Referring to your communication of May 31st . . .	
I have before me your letter dated May 31st . . .	Thank you for your letter of May 31.
Replying to yours of the 31st . . .	
Receipt is acknowledged of yours of the 31st	

Approach the beginning of a letter the same way you approach the beginning of a memo. Address the reader's primary needs. These will differ, depending on your message and your relationship with the reader, but if your beginning meets four fundamental criteria, you'll be sure to start out with a gratified reader:

1. **Identify the subject of your letter.**

2. **Speak directly to the reader, using "you."**

3. **Reach out to your reader's interests.**

4. **Establish a relationship of goodwill.**

For example:

Dear . . . . ,
    I am pleased to let you know the results of the tests you sent us on May 15.

Here, you identify the tests as the subject of your letter. You speak directly to the reader, using *I* and *you*. You refer to the topic of maximum interest to him, since he obviously requested these results. And by saying you're pleased to respond to his request, you immediately establish a relationship of goodwill.

    It's clear and simple!

Now, here are four points for a perfect letter.

1. **Give the good news first. You will put your reader in a positive frame of mind.**

2. **Simply *refer* to the letter you are answering. Don't waste time repeating it in detail. It's enough to write:**
   Here are the copies you requested in your letter of June 19. I hope you will find them useful.

3. **Be consistent in your salutations and signatures. If you're addressing the letter to "Mr. Roland Myers," write "Dear Mr. Myers," *not* "Dear Sir." If you write "Dear Roland," you should sign your letter "David," not "D. Parker" or "David Parker."**

4. **Be easy on the eyes. We read with the eye—and it longs for harmony, space, and variety. Leave at least four spaces *above* the dateline to the letterhead and *below* it to the inside address. Double-space after the inside address, the signature, and the closing paragraph. Double-space between paragraphs, and keep them short. No more than seven lines to a paragraph, just as in the memo.**

23 How to Write a Letter for a Job

Two people with almost identical qualifications apply for a job. One is chosen. Why?

If there was ever a million-dollar question in the minds of businesspeople, this is it. *Why not me?* (If the winner is you, you don't ask questions!) We tend to come up with answers that heap all sorts of prejudices and biases onto the hirer's shoulders—but those answers don't do us much good. After all, his deplorable sexism or favoritism is not our main concern. Our own sad position is. We may fulminate and expostulate and feel better for a moment for doing so. But if we don't get that job, all our sound and fury signify nothing. Worse, our tantrums are apt to get us *de*moted into the playpen. And few people skyrocket from there.

Well, why *not* you? If you have the right qualifications and a wish to do well, you *should* get that job. If you *haven't* got the qualifications, the experience, and a record of hard, imaginative work—there's still hope! I applied for a position in a large public relations firm. I had absolutely no training or experience in PR, yet I got the job. Why? I was told later that a single remark made them decide to "try" me. I had announced boldly to the senior vice-president. "What I lack in experience, I'll make up in enthusiasm!" Apparently he decided that *they needed enthusiasm*—and were willing to take a risk for it.

We're back to other people's needs again, and how *you* can use them to get *your* needs filled. The million-dollar memo secret. It can help you get a job. Let's see how.

First, I want to suggest strongly that you don't rely on lucky guesses. The more good background and experience you can show, the greater your chances of being chosen *because you will be able to fill more needs.* So, before you read on, take a moment to consider your present position. Are you really well qualified for this job? Do you know others who have more to offer? If you were doing the hiring—whom would you choose? If *you* don't think you're the best choice, your chances are pretty slim, no matter how well you state your case! You may need to get more training or experience to be a number one contender.

But if you've got the qualifications — or if you think you've got something good enough to make up for them—pick up a pencil.

MAKING YOUR OWN PROFESSIONAL PROFILE

"Why not me?" Change that "million-dollar question" into a *million-dollar-memo* question: "What do they need?" *They,* of course, are the powers that be — those luminaries who are going to grant you the job. Divide this question into several categories. They need:

A person who can ... (list professional or technical qualifications)

A person who has ... (list the types of experience that would be useful or meaningful)

A person who is ... (list character traits that would be beneficial to the position sought)

Be careful not to make this an autobiography!! You're not trying to prove to yourself that you're Number One. As before, you're trying to find the reader's needs first.

Now look at yourself. What is there about you, your experience, your abilities that fits the ideal candidate just outlined? Go back over everything — and if it fits, put it down in the appropriate category. Keep working on this until you look impossible to ignore, in at least one category. Take heart — you'll be surprised at the good things about yourself you'll turn up!

You have just written down the content of your letter of application. The purpose of that piece of communication will be simply to show the reader that you have what he needs. How well you do that depends on your mastery of techniques of persuasion, your tone, and your style.

YOUR LETTER OF APPLICATION — THE GENTLE ART OF PERSUASION

Persuasion is like happiness—if you make a big fuss about it, you lose it. A persuasive letter is actually one that makes your reader feel it is to *his* advantage to do what you want him to do. Instead of trying to *persuade* him to give you a job, concentrate on showing him what, specifically, you can do for him.

Make your opening paragraph a statement of something specific you have done that makes you perfect for the position offered. *Don't* start by saying "I am applying for the position of ..." So are all the other 900 applicants. That statement will hardly persuade your reader to pay special attention to your letter! Instead, look back to the profile you made up and find the achievement that is most likely to demonstrate that you fit the needs of this job:

As an account executive in XYZ Corporation I tripled the company's billings on two major accounts. (For a position as manager, with some financial/budgetary responsibilities.)

As an account executive in XYZ Corporation I wrote a regular column on financial planning for BCD Investment Bankers, a client of mine. (For a position as financial writer on a newspaper.)

After you've caught the reader's interest with your opening, add one or two more selling points about yourself. (Save a few for your resume!) Then say simply that you're interested in the position he is offering and can be reached at . . .

This clear and simple letter will grab your reader by the lapels. He knows enough about you to want to know more. And when you come in for the interview, you will already stand out as "the one who tripled the billings." Your chances for success are high even before you start talking.

24 How to Write a Complaint Letter That Gets Results

It would be great if communication were always a joyous sharing of needs, with readers disposed to embrace our views and recommendations . . . and demands. Unfortunately, neither life nor business is that simple. Things happen to enrage us. To embarrass us. To make us simply have to say no.

The question is, of course, how we say it.

And that's usually the last question we ask ourselves when we're mad! We rage, "I'm-mad-as-hell-and-I'm-not-going-to-take-it-anymore!" And that's what we end up writing.

The trouble is, mad-as-hell letters rarely produce the results we want. The reader, feeling attacked, responds in kind. He may dig in his heels and refuse to budge on principle. Or he may decide to defend himself vigorously. A ripsnorting exchange of letters may ensue. But unless you were after a dose of adrenaline, you won't get what you want very quickly.

So — what do you do when you're mad?

WRITE A MAD-RAG

If you're like me, you can't be reasonable and mad at the same time. And you're mad! For me, the only way to start a complaint letter is to write down everything I feel. I take a fresh sheet of paper, roll it furiously into the typewriter, and give my anger and self-righteousness full vent. It feels marvelous! I tell the offending individual what I think of him, his company, his pathetic lack of brains. I heap up insults with glorious abandon. I try to be cleverly nasty. I don't stop until I've expended every ounce of my rage.

Then I'm ready to write my letter.

Does this sound dramatic . . . childish . . . unbusinesslike . . . unnecessary? Well, anger *is* dramatic and childish. It's certainly not businesslike. But it seems to be necessary to every human being, and like murder, "it will out." Even if you try to keep it in.

By giving way to my anger, letting it run its course, I help dissipate it. I don't allow it to control my communication—which it would do, were it still buried somewhere inside. Amazingly enough, I can even derive some creative pleasure from it, as I try to write the *most* derogatory, castigating, wry insults ever produced!

I don't throw away all my mad-rags. I keep some for fun, and others to show me how ridiculous I look when I let anger take over. Rereading them, I can imagine how *I* would react if anyone sent me a letter expressing these feelings. I would want to send one right back!

I. *strongly* suggest that you write your own mad-rags. I believe Horace is right when he claims, "Anger is a short madness." And insanity never produced a good letter.

======= Here's a mad-rag to use as an example: =======

You brainless incompetent,

Paragraph one: unprintable epithets and creative curses

I can't believe a company of XXX's stature would hire such a nincompoop as you. Here we are up to our necks in unemployment lines, and people like you are actually drawing regular paychecks. It rocks the mind.

Do you remember, you half-witted turkey, that I talked to you *personally* three times last week? I told you YYY had sent me a package for overnight delivery through your firm at the beginning of the week. Are you aware that people use your "Overnight Delivery Service" precisely because they expect *overnight delivery?* Do you remember that my package had not arrived by Wednesday, Thursday, or Friday?

You said magnanimously that you would "put a tracer on it." I'm ready to put a tracer on you, you grandiloquent fool, and strangle you with my bare hands.

Oh yes, I got the package today. Only *it was the wrong package. My* package consisted of manuscripts. The one in my hands contains several pieces of hardware which I would gladly put to use on your witless skull.

Find my package, Mr._____, and get it to me by special messenger *today*—or I will get the police after you for tampering with the mail.

Yours truly amazed at the immensity of your uselessness,
Cheryl Reimold

Mad-rags like this one give your anger an outlet. They also show why you should never write to someone in the heat of rage. Why? Very simply, the subject of your complaint gets lost in the hubbub. You insult your reader —your reader retaliates—and very soon it becomes a point of honor *not* to cooperate. By the time you both simmer down, the package will be halfway to Kalamazoo.

Furthermore, you end up making a lot of rather stupid remarks when you're mad. I couldn't get the police after my bungling private delivery man for tampering with the U.S. mail. There hadn't been any U.S. mail! And just aesthetically—being up to the neck in unemployment lines suggests an image of thousands of Lilliputians eddying around one looking for work. Not a stimulating or valid metaphor.

Perhaps you're thinking, "Yes, I can see the value of not letting anger control my pen. But who has the time to waste writing a letter that'll never be sent? I'd just go outside and curse at the guy silently for five minutes. Isn't that just as good?"

No. For a mad-rag offers you a chance to do more than just burn off your rage. First, it helps you get all your complaint on paper. When your anger's at a peak, you're not likely to forget any of the details that made you mad. Later, you might.

Second, the mad-rag gives you a unique chance to see the problem in a more realistic perspective. Rereading it, you visualize the idiot who caused you all this trouble, yes. But you also see the letter writer bouncing up and down in a rage, mixing metaphors, and throwing empty punches. Slowly—both parties look just a little ridiculous. And then—just a little human.

That's when you're ready to settle down and write the letter that will get you results.

COMPLAIN WITH STYLE: SEVEN RULES

Now that your anger's soothed, you can safely ask yourself the question, *What do I want?* By now, the answer won't be "To string that idiot up by his ears." Rather, you'll see that you want your problem corrected. And your letter should be focused on getting the reader to correct it for you.

We're right back to the secret of the million-dollar memo. You'll get your needs filled by filling those of your reader. Even if you're convinced that your reader is brainless, deceptive, crooked, or what have you—the rule remains the same. Reach out to him, try to meet his human needs, and he's far more likely to do his best for you.

Here are seven rules to help you complain with panache and success!

1. Think of "a nicely spoken letter." Imagine that you are sitting down to talk with this person who has caused you so much grief and that he or she turns out to be a human being—only a little better than Attila the Hun, but still a human being. Put aside your preconceptions or bad experiences with him. Just imagine, for this one pleasant moment, that he has been transformed into someone with whom you could picture yourself spending a few hours. *Invest* him with qualities he may or may not have. He won't mind your treating him as if he were good, kind, honest, wise. In fact, you may very well flatter him into fleeting contact with those sleeping traits inside him! *Don't start writing* until you've got a firm image of that cozy scene of the two of you chatting amicably. That image is your key to success. Do whatever is necessary — even picturing the presence of someone you really do like instead — to bring it about.

2. Speak to your reader as you would have him speak unto you if *you'd* made a hash of things. We all do, you know. We're human beings. Think back to the last time you gave someone legitimate cause to complain. You probably didn't mean to do it. Most likely you were eager to right the unfortunate wrong. Most people are.

Approach your reader with the conviction that he didn't mean to make this mistake—and believe it. Even if he was really "out to get you," you will disarm him by treating him as if he were above such base instincts.

And notice, at the beginning of this section I said, "*Speak* to the reader." Send him a nicely *spoken* letter. That means you could literally say your letter out loud and sound completely natural.

If you write as you speak naturally (not when you're putting on airs!), you will avoid the monstrosities that plague all business letters. Inflated impersonal expressions such as:

We regret to advise that . . .
Upon investigation we find that . . .
This is to inform you that . . .
We anticipate that we will not be in a position to . . .

Wordy mouthfuls like these beckon to writers of complaint letters. Why?

First, we hope to hide our anger behind the mask of impersonality. If we haven't written any mad-rags, that anger is still there, itching to wield the pen. Stock phrases cover it up.

Of course, if you've written a mad-rag, *you're* now in control. You've let your anger speak. Now you can write fearlessly, in your own words.

Then there's another attraction. We think great gobs of business language make us sound important. Fearsome, even. We've got the whole weight of the business community behind us, symbolized in those few little clichés. The reader wouldn't dare disobey.

But he would. He's got a million "business letters" in his In box. Why should he pay special attention to yours?

Try talking to him, instead. Show human goodwill. It works.

3. Show the reader what's in it for him. Stress the benefits that he will derive by doing as you ask. Don't threaten. Empty threats weaken your argument and encourage the reader to fight you rather than help you.

Instead of saying "Forget about any more business from us" (even if you couch it in politer terms)—tell him you have enjoyed doing business with him and look forward to placing more orders. Provided this one is filled *pronto*. Don't be afraid to inject a note of humor. Chances are you are writing to someone who didn't cause the trouble all by himself. Your tone of goodwill will assure him that you understand his limited reponsibility. *But*—by showing him that he can look like a hero and benefit personally by clearing up the mess, you'll give him two powerful reasons to do your bidding, *now*.

4. Don't be sarcastic. Sarcasm sounds *so* clever on your own lips—and so horribly vicious when it's directed against you. Sarcasm is irony motivated by scorn. It come from the Greek verb *sarcazo,* which means "to tear flesh." That's what it feels like. And it doesn't work for you.

Look at these two requests:

> I'd appreciate a call on this by the end of the week—that is, if your busy schedule of lunches and golf dates permits.

> Would you give me a call this week to discuss this problem? I'm sure we can work it out simply and effectively.

Which request would encourage you to pick up the phone?

5. Give a thorough description of the problem. Impossible as it may seem, you may be part of the cause of the trouble! You may not have given your instructions clearly. You may have omitted certain important details. I was once absolutely livid with a travel agent who had lost me an important flight through sheer inefficiency. I had told her exactly where I wanted to go and the time I wanted to leave. When I arrived at the airport, there was no plane. There *was* a plane leaving at that time for my destination from an airport at the other end of the city. I couldn't, and didn't, make it. Well, I wrote and sent her a mad-rag to end them all. How could she have failed to tell me the name of the airport where I would find my plane? Her answer: "You didn't ask me. I thought you knew."

Perhaps, indeed, she should have told me. But that's not the point. If I had thought to ask *which* airport, the problem would not have occurred.

So, accepting that you might have been remiss in telling or asking something, make sure you tell your reader exactly what you want in your complaint letter. Don't behave as if you were talking to a child. But do assume that your reader will look no further than your letter for details of what went wrong. Be sure they're all there.

6. If possible, give the reader a choice. It may be impossible for him to fulfill your demands as stated, even though he is at fault. All your ranting and raging won't make it possible. Remember, your object is to *get the problem solved,* not to win points. If your reader is too muddleheaded to sort out all your figures before next month, recognize and accept that fact. You can't change it. Instead, offer him the alternative of sending you half the information now, half in a month's time. Half is better than none! And you will have encouraged that particular reader to comply with your request, by showing understanding of his plight.

7. Be courteous, calm, and firm. A calm tone establishes authority—yours. Courtesy is essential to any type of communication other than mudslinging. And slinging mud just gets you more mud. But don't confuse courtesy with hesitancy. Your reader needs to know that you will respond with goodwill and perhaps more orders if he takes care of the problem. But he must also understand that you do not intend to sit smiling courteously if he does nothing. Decide what you will do if he does not comply. Make sure it is realistic and within your power (seeing him become a prisoner of the Ayatollah might be a joy but is probably something you can't accomplish). You may or may not want to tell him what it is. If you intend to act before a certain date, he should know. But otherwise, it's really enough that *you* know you will take action. Your sense of resolution will come through.

Here is a list of the seven rules:

1. Think of a nicely spoken letter.

2. Speak to your reader as you would have him speak to you.

3. Show the reader what's in it for him.

4. Don't be sarcastic.

5. Give a thorough description of the problem.

6. If possible, give the reader a choice.

7. Be courteous, calm, and firm.

PUTTING THE RULES INTO PRACTICE

Now let's put the rules into practice and transform a turn-off letter of complaint into a pleasant, personal message that gets results.

Here's the original:

January 18, 1983

Mr. Samuel Wilkins
_____ Bank
35 Pine Street
Cleveland, OH 05832

Dear Mr. Wilkins,
This in reference to the recent MasterCard bill, charged to my account, dated Jan. 15.

82

It is to my considerable distress that I discover that the problems I have brought to your attention have not been properly corrected. Although the incorrect bill has been removed, there has been no modification to the finance charge.

I would be most grateful if you would oblige me by attending to this matter at your earliest convenience.

Yours sincerely,
John Pearson

The only blunder this letter does not commit is actual rudeness. It is impersonal. It is certainly "unspoken." And above all, it is hopelessly unclear. The writer does not specifiy what charge had been incorrectly billed to his account. He doesn't name the item. He doesn't give a date of charge. He doesn't even give his account number. At the end of the letter, we still do not know what the finance charge is for, what charges have been corrected, or whether there is a connection between the finance charge and these mistaken charges. Finally, after having written three curt, unfriendly paragraphs, John Pearson goes all soft and undemanding. The only reason the reader has for "obliging" Mr. Pearson is to earn his gratitude. Judging from the letter, that will be lukewarm at best.

The tone of the letter is utterly offputting. It translates roughly to "Oh, now I've got to write to that lamebrain who mucked up the Master-Card bill. I don't have time to go rooting through my files for all the details. Let him do it—he's the one who messed up. Serve him right to give him some extra work. I'd better get the thing off so I can get back to my work."

As observers, we may fully sympathize with Mr. Pearson's feelings. We'd probably have them too. But our sympathy and Pearson's indignation *won't get him what he wants:* a corrected statement, with all finance charges removed.

Let's climb into John Pearson's desk chair and rewrite him a letter to get results.

First, the mad-rag.

Dear Half-Wit Wilkins,

It's guys like you that give me migraines. Because of you, Sapless Sammy, I will spend more hard-earned money on another visit to my neurologist in search of expensive chemical relief—when all I need is to be rid of incompetents like you. Don't worry—my doc takes Master-Card.

I just can't believe how you could totally mess up a job. I'm talking about the ludicrous statement your backward computer keeps spitting out at me. *I'm* not about to go through the problem again. You've wasted enough of my time already. Just hang your mindless body over your filing cabinet and pull out the file labeled "Pearson, J."—if you can read. I want a corrected statement and a personal apology from you, pudding-head. If I don't get it, your president is going to get a personal letter from *me*—and it ain't going to paint you in roses, baby. Also I will withdraw all my accounts from the bank and will tell my friends—who are many and influential—to do the same.

> Sincerely urging you to take a flying leap,
> John Pearson

Okay. The adrenaline's provided its good shot of extra energy, the anger is fairly well dissipated, and we can start on the letter.

Step 1: Think of a nicely spoken letter. Sit down comfortably with the imagined Mr. Wilkins. Paint him in pleasant hues. Make him ready to please but perhaps a little scatterbrained.

Sam Wilkins sits nervously on the edge of his chair, waiting for the ax to strike and preparing to defend himself. Instead, you smile at him and think to yourself that he might actually be a nice guy.

Step 2: Speak to him as you would have him speak to you, if the positions were reversed. Instead of attacking, start out with praise. His bank must have done something right, or you wouldn't have chosen its credit card. As you start talking, you can combine steps 2 and 3. You can put Wilkins at ease and treat him with respect (step 2), and you can show him what's in it for him (step 3). For instance:

> I must tell you how pleased I have been with my _____ Bank MasterCard. Your fees are still the lowest around, and I was delighted to note that you have increased my credit limit to $3,000.

Now Samuel Wilkins starts to behave differently. He's neither poised to attack nor anxious to flee. He's expectant. If he plays it right, he may even be commended for straightening out the problem.

It's time to move on to steps 4 and 5. Give him a thorough description of the problem with no sarcastic overtones. Forget about what you've told him before. Just tell him what's wrong now.

> I was glad to see that you have removed the charge for the Eastern Airlines ticket, billed to my account 754-82-9503 on October 15, 1982. As I told you, I canceled that trip and had requested credit on my MasterCard. However, the charge of $881.72 remained on my November 1982 and December 1982 statements. While I waited for the charge to be removed, the finance charges on it kept building up.

> Now—my problem is the finance charge. It has not been removed. On the contrary—it has now gone up to $59.68.

Now tell him what you want him to do. Give him a choice, if possible (step 6).

84

As you can imagine, I would like this finance charge removed from my credit record as soon as possible. A letter from you confirming its removal would give me great peace of mind.

If that is difficult, please do see that it is taken off my next statement. But—I would appreciate a letter.

Now the closing paragraph—courteous, calm, but firm (step 7).

I realize that computer errors can happen in an operation the size of yours. I'm sure I can depend on you to resolve my problem quickly— and I look forward to receiving a letter from you soon.

And there's your letter. You began by reaching out and filling Mr. Wilkins's needs. You praised his bank and hinted, by your tone, that you would continue to be a valued customer if he behaved himself. Then you told him clearly and simply what the difficulty was. And you enlisted his help. This letter will neither enrage nor perplex him. He will be eager to do all he can to keep your goodwill and your business.

If you follow this method, you won't have any more "difficult" letters to write. Suppose you have to write a delicate refusal. Or a request for financial aid. Or even a defense of your own unpopular position on something. Just remember to sit down with your reader (in your mind) and approach him as a colleague rather than an adversary. Talk to him as if you were two intelligent, friendly human beings who *both* want to resolve the problems.

Begin your conversation, and your letter, by reaching out into the common ground between you. Say something positive. Make him feel that this communication is on the up rather than the down side. Make him feel you trust him.

Then, describe the problem in detail. *Don't* be falsely apologetic, ingratiating, promising, threatening, or sarcastic. You can spot a lie a mile off, can't you? So can your reader.

Close with a courteous but firm statement of your intentions.

In this letter you will have met at least two of your reader's basic human needs. You will have shown him respect. And you will have given him the precise, complete knowledge he needs to get to work. There will be no additional friction between you to add another problem to the one you are trying to resolve.

Here are a few wrap-up points to remember:

When you write a complaint letter, *remember:*

• **You write a complaint letter *to get a problem solved*—not to trade curses and insults.**

- Letters written in anger *obscure the subject of the complaint.* The writer is so busy heaping up abuse and the reader so fuming with resentments that the subject itself gets lost.

- *Empty threats are boomerangs.* They will turn against you when you can't carry them out. *You* will be the one who looks ridiculous.

- Sarcasm stings. Remember Jonathan Swift: "Whoever is out of patience is out of possession of his soul. Men must not turn into bees who kill themselves in stinging others."

WHAT TO DO IF YOU STILL GET NO RESPONSE

What if your courteous letter does not produce results? What if Sam Wilkins is in fact the chairman's nephew who doesn't need the job and couldn't care less about your mounting finance charges?

If his action is not immediate—send him a copy of your letter as a reminder. But if another month goes by, and your credit rating is in danger, it's time for different action.

You have a choice. Either send Sam Wilkins a note warning him that you are now going to write to the president of the bank and/or the Better Business Bureau. Or simply write to the president and send a copy to the delinquent Wilkins.

Whatever you do, don't waste emotion on it. Just make it clear and simple.

If you're giving Sam another chance, write simply:

Dear Mr. Wilkins,

The erroneous finance charge on my account 754-82-9503 has not been removed. I have written to you repeatedly about this, but you have done nothing to correct the mistake. The charge is now $101.

I shall now have to take up this matter with your president. Unless I hear from you by the end of the week, I shall write to him of your grossly inadequate performance and to demand satisfaction from him. If I don't get an immediate response, I shall write to the Better Business Bureau to inform them of the delinquent practices of you personally as well as the bank you represent.

Sincerely,
John Pearson

I have never had to write this final letter. Clarity, courtesy, and goodwill have won me the same in return, in all my dealings so far.

25 How—and When—to Write for a Raise

If you're getting itchy about your job and you want a raise or a promotion, you have two options. One, you can wait around and hope that you get it. Two, you can go and see your boss about it.

If you do nothing, you are leaving your fate entirely in your boss's hands. If you go to see him, you're giving yourself an extra chance to shine.

MAKING YOUR VALUE KNOWN

Before you march in, remember the secret of the million-dollar memo. Fill someone's needs—and he's very likely to fill yours.

So don't go telling your boss why you deserve a promotion. That's *your* need. Tell him you have some ideas for a couple of interesting projects. Outline them. Ask him if you can put them in a memo to him—if he hasn't already asked you to do that.

Before you write that memo—pause again. You know your boss. Will he resent your telling him why you should be promoted? If so—don't. Tell him your ideas, using all your million-dollar memo techniques. Tell him how *you* would put them into effect. And leave it at that. He'll be pleased, interested, impressed. That's fine.

But if you think your boss will be ready to listen to cogent reasons for promoting you—read on.

PUTTING IT IN WRITING

For this memo, give yourself time. Write out a dialogue with your boss (see Chapter 2). Use the dialogue to do Phase 1 of the million-dollar method. Then, before approaching Phases 2 and 3, prepare the profile suggested at the beginning of Chapter 23. Circle any recent achievements of yours that you can use to give your boss new information. Perhaps some new figures have just come in, or a congratulatory letter. Maybe you have just completed an important phase of a pet project. Try to remind your boss of something outstanding and interesting about yourself in your opening sentence. Something that you have done that fills one of his needs. Remember, the first technique of persuasion is to show your reader what you can do, and are doing, *for him*.

Using this sentence as your starter, go into Phase 2. Write everything you can think of that will interest your reader on your activities so far. Put down your ideas for future activities and projects. When you come to Phase 3, you may well find a unifying force behind all your activities that will show your unique value to the firm.

THE POWER OF ENTHUSIASM

In Phase 3, you will be working to fashion a memo that presents you through your work. Here, bring the next technique of persuasion into play: *enthusiasm*. People who talk about their subjects with animation manage to captivate readers or listeners who may never have given the topics a second thought. Those who don't, don't. I remember a project director who was mumbling through the details of his work to a group of company executives. His facts were all there, and the procedures spelled out clearly. At one point the director looked up from his notes and bleated at this audience, "It's really very exciting." Whereupon a restless vice-president roared in response, "Then for God's sake, get excited about it, man!"

Get excited about your work. Show your reader how important it is to the company and to you. You should have a memo of three to four paragraphs that says proudly: This is what I've been doing. These are my plans for further efforts, and this is what I'm now doing to put them into effect.

STATING YOUR NEEDS

When you reach the final paragraph, tell your reader honestly that you feel ready to take on more responsibility. Say that you hope some of the work you have done speaks for your abilities and creative solutions. If the job you aspire to take has a title, name it specifically. If you feel the job you are doing is really worth $4,000 more per year, name the figure. Your reader may disagree with you—but he will respect and appreciate your honesty. And knowing clearly what you're after, he may be more amenable to negotiation.

Your three techniques of persuasion, then, follow one after another in your final memo. First, you interest the reader by showing that you have what he needs. Second, you further his interest in you and your projects by filling your report with enthusiasm for the work and the company. Third, you gain his respect through your straightforward, honest statement of your own needs. Close with a simple sentence saying you would like to talk with him, at his convenience.

Can you do any more to make this memo a success? Yes—you can make sure your tone is right, your style attractive, and your presentation perfect and neat.

Check your memo to your boss once more. Does the tone say "I respect you"? Is the language clear and simple? Can you perhaps see the beginnings of a personal style?

Great! You have now turned a difficult request into an interesting, appealing memo. Pretty soon that memo or another like it will turn into a new job or a raise.

26 How to Write a Technical Memo

How do you spark your boss with enthusiasm for your particular lab project? If you've read this far, you know already. *Show him how it fills his needs.* And make him feel your own genuine enthusiasm. It's highly infectious.

The way you tell your boss about any technical task you're performing is usually to write a *technical memo* or *report.* A report may sound more complicated, but it is actually just a longer, more detailed technical memo. What is common to both, and what concerns us here, is the special act of translation you have to perform. You have to translate abstruse technical data into compelling English. To do so effectively—and you will—you must first rid your mind of certain common deceptions.

TECHNICAL BOOBY TRAPS

Deception #1. There is a special kind of writing called "technical writing." That's what I have to use for my report. Wrong. You are writing to people who read English, not machines programmed to "read" another special language. The top executives who read your report may have little or no technical background or expertise. Your job is to tell them in clear and simple English what you're doing and why it is important to them.

Deception #2. You write a technical memo or report to keep your superiors informed of your work in progress. Wrong. You *never* write anything in business just to keep people informed. Rather, you tell them first what *they* want to know. To list facts is not enough. You have to tell your readers the significance of these facts *to them.* For instance, it's not enough to write:

> *The pressure on the cable was 50 pounds per square foot.*

You must tell the reader how this fact affects the success or progress of your project:

> *The pressure on the cable was 50 pounds per square foot—enough to test the elasticity of the new material. The cable held firm.*

Now, with or without technical background, the reader knows *why* that pressure was exerted *(to test the elasticity of the new material)* and what significance that part of the test has *(the cable held firm).* You have told your executive reader what *he* wants to know — namely, whether your tests suggest that the company should invest money in this new material.

   Deception #3. A technical memo or report is just a routine part of my work – a chore to be completed because records require it. Wrong, wrong, *wrong.* That report is nothing less than *you and your work on paper.* It's often the only chance you get to tell top management what you are doing, what you have done, and why it is worthwhile. Remember, what you create or discover in the privacy of your office or your lab is useless if you can't explain it to those who are paying you to create or discover.

   Okay. The technical memo or report is crucial to you and your career. Let's see how to write one.

THE SEARCH FOR ELEGANT SIMPLICITY — IN FOUR STEPS

1. *Simplify.* That's your first rule for translation of technical material into good English. Complicated facts *can* be related simply. If you're shaking your head and muttering "You haven't seen what I have to write about," read Sir Isaac Newton's *Laws of Motion:*

> The change of motion is proportional to the motive force impressed. . . .
> To every action there is always opposed an equal reaction. . . .

The laws of the universe — each boiled down to a single, readable sentence. But if Sir Isaac had been corrupted by the techno-verbiage of today, he would have written something like:

> In the case of moving bodies, a modification of kinesis occurs in direct proportion to the extent or amplitude of the amount of force hitherto impressed upon the activated body.

Right?

   Contrast the great scientist's clear and simple expression of the laws of motion with a "technical" description of group therapy that appeared in a recent publication:

> As a result of the verbal interaction of participants, there evolves a collective understanding which in turn stimulates further co-individual responses, coextensive with the newly emerging group behavior. . . .

   Simplify your thoughts. Then, when you're thinking clearly and simply, describe the events or theories to be reported in uncomplicated English. Remember to put just one thought in each sentence. Then your sentences won't need therapy!

2. *Describe the process step by step.* A public relations firm in New York tests would-be copywriters by asking them to write a press release for pliers!

The candidates have to assume that pliers have just been invented. They must write a press release that explains how the tool works and why the reader will benefit from owning one. And they have to interest the reader all the way through.

This is an excellent exercise to prepare you for writing a technical memo or report. Take an hour tonight and try it. Just describe, one step after another, how that simple instrument works. Remember, you want to *interest* as well as inform. So, imagine a reader and decide what would interest *him* about pliers. Tell him that first. Once you've aroused his interest, he'll give you his attention.

For example, suppose your reader is the president of your company. You want to tell him why the company should start manufacturing this new instrument. The president's first question will probably be: Why would people use this? So start by saying something like:

> A new instrument, called *pliers*, enables anyone with minimum strength
> to bend a wire or hold in place or turn small objects, such as nails. Pliers
> will make it possible for millions of people to do their own household
> repairs at the flick of a wrist.

You've got his interest. Now let him *see* the instrument and visualize how it works.

Proceed to describe the instrument so that he can see it clearly for himself. Begin by relating this unknown tool to something familiar to the reader—tweezers and scissors, maybe. Then tell him how it works, step by step. Your purpose is to lead a reader who knows nothing about your subject to a complete understanding of it. So you must keep it simple. Put no more than one idea in a sentence. Keep your sentence structure as uncomplicated as possible.

> Pliers resemble a pair of scissors. They consist of two S-shaped
> pieces of metal. These are set opposite each other and held together
> with a screw.
> The "S" is not even. The handle is about three times as long as the
> tip. And the two pieces have been designed so that the tips *meet* when
> shut, unlike scissors, whose blades cross.
> Now, how do pliers work? To hold a nut while driving in a screw, for
> instance, you simply open the pliers by the handles as you would a pair of
> scissors. Position the tips on either side of the nut. Close the handles.
> The tips, which are slightly grooved, will have a firm grip on the nut.
> Remember, the handles are much longer than the tips. Therefore, the
> principle of leverage enables you to hold the nut in place with much less
> force than you would otherwise have to use. Even when the screw is
> tightened to the maximum, the nut will not move.

Now you try the exercise! Think up a different reader or find a different way to describe the instrument.

At first, you may balk at the difficulty of trying to describe such a simple instrument *simply*. Don't be daunted. You'll find that the hurdles drop as soon as you approach the description *piece by piece* and *step by step*.

When we look at a familiar object, we see it as a single unit. Its appearance, its function, the reason it works that way, and the benefits we derive from it — all these attributes appear to us together and simultaneously. And we have no trouble processing that perception.

The trouble starts when we have to describe the object to someone else. We may assume that the reader knows more about it than he does. So, we leave out important information. Or we may try to describe everything at once—the look, the feel, the workings, the effects. And we get tied up in incoherent, unconnected strings of words.

The way to cut through the confusion is to consider the different qualities of the subject separately. Then approach the description of each quality step by step. *Don't* think about the specific uses of an instrument when you're busy describing its appearance. Just tell your reader what it looks like. You can explain its many uses in another paragraph devoted to *function*.

If you can't lay your hands on a pair of pliers, try describing another simple instrument. An emery board. A ballpoint pen. A lipstick. A pencil sharpener. Any simple tool will do. It will give you the same challenge and training in logical description. Just be sure it *is* a simple tool. No computers or Cuisinarts. It's easy to give up, saying, "No one but an expert could possibly describe an Apple II." But we should all be able to describe a pocket nail file.

Once you've managed that description, you'll be able to present anything clearly, from calculators to complex filing systems. And you'll have the writing tools you need to structure any technical memo or report.

3. *Avoid technical jargon.* Remember Newton's laws. They are all in clear, concise, readable English. Of course there are times when you will have to use a technical word, simply because there is no general English expression for it. But don't fall into the trap of *superspecificity!* Because of their precision training, many technical writers want every word or concept they use to have a single specific meaning. This aim is laudable in the lab, where the technical words are part of the common language. It is ludicrous in a memo to nontechnical readers who can't make head or tail out of a single superspecific term! Keep technological terminology to a minimum. It is far better to be less specific and more widely understood.

4. *Never forget that your purpose is communication, not just presentation.* Clarity, concern for the reader's concerns, a logical structure, and an understandable frame of reference are all tools to help you reach this single all-important goal. To help you do so with very little effort, rig up the sign

COMMUNICATE! in bright lights before your mind's eye.

Okay. You're going to think and write *simply*. If you find yourself getting tied up in preposterous polysyllabics, think of Newton. Or Einstein —$E=mc^2$ (energy equals mass times the speed of light squared). If the principles of the universe can be set down in a few words understandable to a twelve-year-old, so can the principles or events you are describing.

When you describe, describe logically, step-by-step, phase of the project by phase. Focus completely on the step you're describing. Forget about what precedes or follows it. You can make connections clearer later. Just make sure you make each phase understandable—if possible, visible.

Review your description of pliers (or mine, if you haven't done one of your own). Think up a reader and then think like him (Phase 1). Write down everything you know about the subject (Phase 2). Then organize your writing into a report that begins with the attribute most interesting to your reader. Continue with your description as in the model. Use this model for all your technical reports or memos. Make a few copies of it—you'll find it gets dog-eared and underlined quicker than you'd think!

27 How to Write a Highly Readable Technical Report

Like a memo, the technical report must interest the reader and, if possible, answer his questions on the subject.

Get a few 3 x 5 cards. Keep a card for each type of reader. Label each card according to the category of readers your report may reach—management, research, etc. In parentheses, write the name of an actual person who will read your report. For example, you could write the name of the president of the company next to "Management."

Now list the questions that each reader is likely to bring to your report before opening it. If the questions roll into your head one on top of the other, write them down before they roll out again! If you get stuck, try the dialogue suggested in Chapter 2. The questions may be general or specific, depending on the subject of the report. They might run something like this:

MANAGEMENT (John H. Rickles, President)

1. How much has this project cost so far?
2. How much can it be expected to cost?
3. What are the potential profits?
4. When could we begin to see them?
5. Might this work make us more competitive?
6. Could it lead us into a new line?
7. What would be the advantages and disadvantages of getting into that new area?
8. Why should we continue to support and fund this project?

RESEARCH (Michael S. Parks, Research Director)
1. How far has this project progressed?
2. What technical snags has it experienced or overcome?
3. Does it look technologically feasible for us?
4. Is the process or product we are working on here better than those we now have? In what way?
5. Have any new or puzzling facts come to light as a result of this project?

You will want to amend these lists of questions to fit the project, its significance, the history of its acceptance in the company, and the character of certain key readers—the ones you are keeping firmly in mind (and in parentheses).

Once you have written down the questions, answer them. On paper. Take each question of each reader, look up the data you need to answer it, and write down everything you can think of to answer that question quickly and completely.

When you've finished with the questions, close your eyes and think of your projected report. What else do your readers need to know? If other topics come to mind, write them down and, if possible, put in parentheses the type of reader each would interest. Then follow your Phase 2 writing technique. *Just write.* Everything and anything on that topic. Make notations where tables or figures might illustrate or explain your point.

Now you have a number of cards or sheets of paper, each one self-contained. This is what you *should* have—for a technical report is literally a *multi-translation* of your work into several languages, one for each type of reader. Since your readers will vary in interest and background, you must use a different language for each.

THE PYRAMID OF VALUE

Approach your report as a pyramid. Each section is a more detailed amplification of the ones above it. I call the report a pyramid of value, because it is so valuable a record and statement of your work and also because each section, or layer, has a special value for a particular reader. The pyramid of value looks like this:

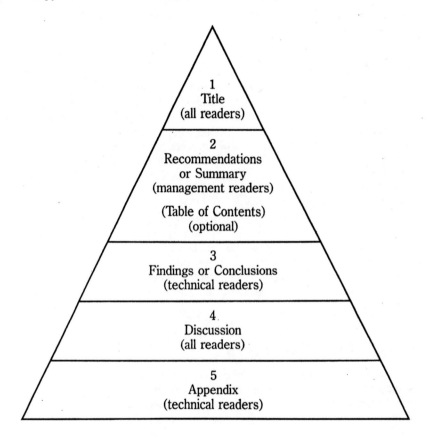

Your report is actually going to be five separate translations of a single event.

THE TITLE

The title is the most general, sweeping, and comprehensive statement of all. It must be clear to everyone who reads it. It must tell, in as few words as possible, the *subject* of your report and *your specific activity* within this subject's bounds. Think of your title as an introduction to an exciting dramatic event—a program note, if you will. It tells:

the subject • the action • the actors • the time • the place

RECOMMENDATIONS

In the section on recommendations you want to sketch a broad outline of the significance of the project to management. Here you recommend support for your project by showing your readers that *they* will find it worthwhile. Look back at your "Management" question card. Management readers will want to know how the company will gain from this work and why that gain is significant. This is the place to tell them—clearly.

If you are not yet at a stage where you can make recommendations, write a *short* summary in which you try to answer as many of the reader's imagined questions as possible.

If you have recommendations to make, write a two-to-three-sentence paragraph on the achievement of the project so far. Then follow with a list of recommendations, placed one under the other with stars (★) or bullets (•) to set them off. Remember, only *one* recommendation to each star or bullet. We can take in only one fact at a time. You are working to lead your reader through your report as clearly and simply as possible. He will thank you for it.

TABLE OF CONTENTS

You might want to insert a table of contents after the recommendations or summary, especially if there are many subsections in the parts to follow. If not, it may be wiser (and clearer) simply to append colored index tabs to mark each section. Imagine that you were receiving the report. Which method would guide you more easily and pleasantly through it? Your reader's interest and comfort should make the decision for you.

FINDINGS

Findings or conclusions should do for technical readers what recommendations did for management. This section should answer their most pressing questions. Here you will list the discoveries you have made on the project, in their order of importance to your technical reader (not necessarily to you). *Do not* be tempted to spin them out so as to get as many as possible! A short page of three or four solid conclusions is more readable, meaningful, *and* impressive than a two-page list of every tiny discovery.

The section on findings or conclusions should also provide the evidence on which you based your recommendations. Can the interested reader fit each recommendation to a finding? If not, add to your findings or conclusions the specific source of that dangling recommendation.

If your findings need calculations or graphs to complete their sense, you can add a couple. But keep the artwork to a minimum here. Your reader wants to be able to scan this section (one page, if possible) for a broad understanding of what is to follow. He expects you to save the details for the discussion.

DISCUSSION

The discussion is really the most fun to write. It's the main section of the report, in which you finally get to tell all your readers about your project. You have tickled their respective fancies in the previous sections. Here is the entree for which you whetted their appetites.

The discussion is literally an amplification of everything you have said so far. It is also the place to answer any remaining questions your readers might have.

Begin by expanding on your recommendations and findings. If you have recommended buying a new part or a new machine, explain here how it will be better than the ones you now have. If there are terms or processes that may not be clear to the management reader, define them. Explain any calculations used in your tests. Refer to any appended figures that illustrate your studies or discoveries.

You will help your reader follow your discussion if you give each recommendation or finding a subhead. Just make it a shorter version of the recommendation itself. Then treat each of these subsections as if it were a "pliers" exercise. Explain what your readers need to understand step by step, one thought to a sentence, in simple, uninflated English. If you use a technical term, define it immediately. You will find you have all the material you need on your question cards and papers. Now you are shaping it into a linear, logical explanation.

You may find that the information you are using to explain some of your recommendations or findings is the same as that which you have already used to explain others. In that case, combine the two or more into one umbrella subhead and explain how your details support each one.

When you are satisfied that you have answered all your readers' potential questions, look back at your cards and papers from Phase 2 writing. Cross out all the material you have translated into the report. Decide whether the remaining information is necessary or valuable to any of your readers. Be ruthless here. Remember, you can harm yourself by telling your readers things they don't care about. They will eventually tune you out altogether.

So make your information pass that "reader need" test before you include it in your report. If it does, make up a new subhead that corresponds to the need you're answering (that will *force* you not to kid yourself) and tell your readers what they need to know.

A DISCUSSION CHECKLIST

You will see that your discussion actually consists of many small discussions on different topics of interest to different people. Look at the organization of these subsections. Have you begun with the topic of greatest interest to the greatest number—or the most influential—of your readers? Is the next topic the next in order of importance, and so on down the line? It's far too easy to organize the report according to the topics of most interest to *you!* But you're not writing the report *to you*. Right?

Approve or change the order of your subsections. Then, for each one, test for:

- *Significance.* Can you name the readers who will be interested in what you have to say here?

- *Coherence.* Have you described the topic or process step by step, leaving out no crucial link? Have you led your reader carefully from ignorance to understanding?

- *Emphasis.* Have you told the reader what was important in this process?

- *Comprehensiveness.* When describing something, have you *named* it, told *how it works, compared it* to something the reader knows, and let the reader see it *part by part?*

And cut out any:

- *technical terms that could be translated into plain English*

- *excessive explanation (elaboration of the obvious)*

- *phony fancies . . . nounery . . . passive voice constructions . . . wasted words . . . grammatical gaffes*

COMMON PROBLEMS WITH REPORTS

Now you should have a sleek, complete, immensely readable report. Do you know how rare that is? Most of the reports that come my way for doctoring or deep surgery suffer mostly in the discussion section. The most common problems are:

- *Density.* The whole discussion section seems to be black type, with no relief but the margins. Paragraphs are endless. Subsections don't exist. Just to look at this mass of reading matter is offputting. It takes real courage to try to read it.

- *Lack of humanity.* Actions "are performed"; we never see anyone actually doing them. The passive voice and impersonal constructions run rampant across the dark, deadly type.

- *Techno-verbiage.* If the writer attempted to use English in the earlier sections of the report, he considers that he's done his duty. In the discussion he gives rein to maximum technical verbosity, seeming at times to be setting paragraph against paragraph to see which can accumulate the most words of limited currency and limitless syllables.

- *Haphazard organization.* Subsections, if there are any, follow no order. The writer just puts down everything be knows at whatever point it occurs to him. This is fine for Phase 2—but Phase 2 without Phase 3 is like a bowl of batter that no one has baked. The cake you were hoping for isn't there.

THE APPENDIX

Your report is really finished with your discussion section. Paradoxically, however, the longest part of the document is often its "attachment"—the appendix. Here you copy and include all the technical information—charts, tables, diagrams, transcripts of papers or speeches, a selected bibliography—that the technical reader with a great interest in the subject will want to peruse. The appendix is also a source of references for anyone eager to learn more about a certain point. That is why you should refer to it when relevant in the body of your report.

I said that each section of the report was nothing less than a separate *translation* of the project. The title is a one-line description of the project. The recommendations present the essence of the project to management. The findings present the essence to technical readers. The discussion tells everybody what he wants to know about the project. And the appendix is really the event telling itself—in documents.

If you remember

(1) to write each section for the assumed reader of that section,
(2) to keep sections separate,
(3) *not* to repeat yourself from one section to another, and
(4) to answer the readers' questions,

you will write a real million-dollar report!

PART VI

THE MILLION-DOLLAR METHOD IN BRIEF

Make yourself necessary to somebody.
                              Ralph Waldo Emerson

The King went on, "I shall never, never forget!"
  "You will, though," the Queen said, "if you don't
make a memorandum of it."
                              Lewis Carroll

28 Think Differently

The secret of the million-dollar memo is now yours, as well as the "magic" techniques to make it happen. I say "magic," because that's how it will feel, at first. When I started writing like this, I really began to feel that my pen or my IBM must be bewitched. Otherwise—how could I be writing so much faster? And why on earth were people to whom I had written complaint letters suddenly sending me refunds?? One very kind gentleman—whom I have never met—actually called me to apologize for his organization's dilatory tactics. He said, "I told them if they want me to stay on here, they'd better get moving on it!" I was flabbergasted. But it happened.

Why did it happen? I didn't find any genies hiding in my typewriter. No, I believe it was simply the underlying million-dollar memo secret at work. I chose to assume that my readers were honest, caring human beings who had every right to be treated as such. I tried to fill as many of their human needs as possible. They responded by trying to fill mine.

After a while, million-dollar writing will become natural to you. You won't even have to think about what to do, in which order, or how to put it all together. But for the first six months or so you'll find it useful to have an outline of the method at your side. And after that—there will still be occasions. Times when the old "business-writing" tape starts to play, of its own accord, in your head. Moments when you just feel like being stuffy and pompous and hugely important. Other moments when you want to tear out someone's hair and haven't the patience to do it in a mad-rag. Then you'll need my book again—especially this chapter, which gives you the million-dollar method in brief. It's clear and simple.

Good writing flows from good thinking. To write the clear and simple memo that will speed you to the top, you must first change your thinking, in three ways.

THINK: I WANT TO TALK TO SOMEONE

With a single thought—"I want to talk to someone"—you free yourself of all the heavy baggage you've accumulated over the years of exposure to "business language." The words that come to your mind to express your thoughts will be good, clear, honest words that will immediately speak to those qualities in your reader. You will be in little danger of producing the preposterous kind of "business writing" that arrived on my desk the other day. It was a letter from a company that had apparently taken over my health insurance company. Sentence #1 informed me of "a merger which had been effected" between my original health insurers and the people behind this letter. Sentence #2 read:

> This merger was proposed in direct response to M.H.P.'s loss of federal qualification as a Health Maintenance Organization (H.M.O.) and the rehabilitation proceeding involving M.H.P. brought by the Superintendent of Insurance of the State of New York following a finding by the Superintendent that M.H.P. was insolvent and that without outside management and financial assistance, continued operations could adversely affect its policy holders.

Would you believe that, after hitting me with this incomprehensible monstrosity, the letter writer went on to assume that I would be delighted with the news? That I would rejoice in becoming "a subscriber of the largest N.Y.S. certified H.M.O."? All *I* felt was ill—and I certainly didn't trust this new company to take care of my health care costs (even though the present attack was merely a case of bad letteritis!). But seriously, I thought: These people can't even put a clear sentence together in a letter whose purpose is to woo and calm a potential subscriber. How clear are they about my rights and responsibilities? How can I hope to understand their claim forms and procedures? Should I continue to subscribe?

And my answer was no. I didn't trust these people. I found another company, with whom I am still insured. That letter alone managed to lose the organization one person's regular premiums.

I mention this letter and my reaction to it to illustrate the enormous power bad business writing can have. You just can't afford to do it anymore!

THINK: I WANT TO COMMUNICATE

We are social beings. We rejoice in company in a birth, and we come together to give solace in a death. One of our primary needs is to step out of our own perceived "alone-ness" and make contact, join company, with another person.

Yet in business, people behave as if this were not so. Somehow, a type of verbiage has evolved that keeps people from reaching one another. It is as if someone had set down a law saying, *Use words that will keep your reader at a safe distance.*

What happens? You put thick verbal hedges all around you, so no one can see what you're thinking or if—God forbid!—you made a mistake.

We have been conditioned to mistrust each other, in business. We feel that if we speak and act honestly, someone will take advantage of us or show us up as less than perfect. So we hide behind business language. When you write "As per your request, enclosed please find . . . ," you divest yourself and your reader of simple humanity. You both become impersonal beings—faceless, soulless, certainly humorless. And nobody shines.

But—if you want to shine . . . if you want to be remembered and approved . . . if you want to have your million-dollar needs filled . . . you have to communicate. You have to reach out and try to fill your reader's needs first. Find out what's common between you. Talk about it. Let your reader know it's a pleasure to be in touch with him—*before* you give him all that crucial information. When you give it, make it complete but readable, telling him only what *he* needs to know.

When you reach out, your reader will respond by reaching out to you. Just as people meet hedging by covering up themselves, so they meet honesty with frankness. If you take responsibility for your actions and say what you mean, you'll find your readers will do the same. It's great—and it works.

THINK LIKE YOUR READER

Imagine yourself behind your reader's desk, receiving your memo. Jot down the four questions that will help you write the kind of memo that reader will read:

- *Who* will read this?

- *Why* would he bother to read it?

- *What* specific problems or needs of his can it answer?

- *How* can it meet these needs?

Once you've got the *who* firmly in mind—including the particular character, interests, and personality of the reader—you can use the remaining questions to form the basis for your free-flowing writing (Phase 2). When you come to that phase, you may choose to work out a dialogue between you and your reader or to write sections headed by topics of interest to the reader. I always like to start with a dialogue, because it seems to get a more natural style flowing.

Before you start writing, though, review the list of basic human needs that you will try to meet in your memo:

- **Companionship—you will write as one agreeable human being talking with pleasure to another**

- **Approval—you will show your reader that you value him and his opinions**

- **The pleasure of a job well done—you will try to find a way to help the reader in his work**

- Mental stimulation—you will assume your reader is intelligent and you will share your knowledge and excitement about your topic with him

- Discovery and broadening of knowledge—you will bother to give your reader all the details he needs to fill this need

- Aesthetic satisfaction—you will make a memo of varied sentence structure, accurate grammar, clear and simple language, and neat appearance.

So before you start writing, think:

1. I want to talk to ...

2. I want to communicate with him.

3. I want to think like him.

29 Write Differently

By changing your way of thinking, you have already changed the focus of your written message. You still have the same thing to say—but now you will concentrate on making it as attractive and accessible as possible to your particular readers. Within that reader-focused framework, you can start to write differently.

WRITE FREELY AND CEASELESSLY

Write a dialogue between you and your reader, as in Chapter 2. Or write down topics and questions of interest to your reader and answer them. Or note down the subjects you want to cover on a separate card and just start writing, wherever you feel like beginning. So long as you have your reader's needs and interests firmly in mind, the format you choose doesn't matter.

Start writing. Write everything you know or feel like saying about the topic or question. When you come to the end of the questions, write down ·anything else that *you* feel is important. Write, write, write. You'll be amazed at how much you have to say.

But don't make one correction. Absolutely not one. A single pause to change a word or cross out an expression will hold back this part of your work. You see, you are trying to give your creative faculties full, unfettered freedom. Stopping to edit is like pausing in the middle of a great leap to tie a shoelace.

Don't even worry about throwing in some pompous puffery. If you've been strewing *herewith*s and *reference-is-made-to-your-letter-of*s about your pages for the past umpteen years, you can't expect them to blow away. However unnatural they may be in speech, these expressions may by now be a part of your writing vocabulary. Don't worry about them. You can clear them up later. For now, your *sole* purpose is to get all your knowledge, thoughts, and discoveries down on paper. You can do that only if you write freely and without concern for the quality of the writing itself.

FIND YOUR UNIFYING FORCE

Look over your complete, unedited piece of writing. Ask yourself one question: What do I really want to convey? Think back to the Gettysburg

107

Address, and Lincoln's unchanging impetus to save the Union. What is the force behind your writing? Why are you writing this?

Then go through your pages with your purple pencil.

30 Make It Clear and Simple

The focus and the organization of your memo are now clear and simple. You're focusing on your reader's needs. You're presenting your message (the unifying force) in the way that most interests your reader. You will begin with your reader's greatest concern—not your own—and you will structure the memo around your reader's needs.

Now you can turn to the words themselves. I wish I could give you a long magnifying glass with the words CLEAR AND SIMPLE engraved on it! You would put it across every line of your draft, and it would be the test for every word and expression you use. Even without that aid, however, you soon will automatically apply this criterion to your writing, and you will know a muffled monster when you see it.

Here are a few guidelines for getting rid of the chaff:

WRITE WHAT YOU MEAN

If you can "translate" any of your written expressions into a clearer and simpler phrase—use that clear and simple phrase. It's what you mean to say. Say it.

For now, you should subject every sentence you've written to this scrutiny. Look at it and say: What do I mean here? If you've said it better in your answer to that question, write down the answer.

A budget director sat down to define "short-term projects." He wrote:

Short-term projects are those that have an anticipated termination within a period of months or years, the term commensurate with the support given.

If he had looked hard at that monstrosity and asked himself "What do I mean?" he would probably have answered:

Short-term projects are those that last as long as their support allows.

A report of a traffic safety council declares:

While it has been impossible to pinpoint statistically the fact that mechanical failure is responsible for accidents, there is a growing consensus of opinion that this is definitely the case.

109

What did the writer mean, in clear and simple English?

Although we cannot prove statistically that mechanical failure causes accidents, it certainly appears to contribute to them.

Why did those writers produce those muddled mouthfuls instead of clear and simple statements? There are a number of reasons, including force of habit, but I think the most significant is the *fear* of writing a clear and simple statement. If you say something clearly, you can't claim that you were misunderstood. There's no room for hedging. You have to be ready to stand behind your statement and vouch for its validity. You have to be confident of yourself and your knowledge. That confidence is translated in the clear and simple statement you dare to make.

If you are promoting someone — would it be the self-confident, straightforward person who uses words to transmit, not efface, his message? Or would it be the hedger ... the word-wringer ... the person who has to use dozens of words to muddle his message and give himself an "out" in case he's made a mistake?

Clear and simple. It's the million-dollar way.

USE ACTION VERBS

Avoid the state-of-being verbs as much as possible. Those are the connectives that *don't show anyone doing anything*. The most common are the forms of "to be" and "to have."

Look at the original outpourings of the budget director and the traffic safety official. In the first, the only verbs are *are* and *have*. No action verbs. In the second, we find *has been, pinpoint, is, is, is*. Only *one* action verb (*pinpoint*) in a mouthful of 30 words.

Remember, your writing is supposed to transmit concepts from your mind to the reader's. The most effective way to grasp a concept is to see it. You don't "see" abstractions. You do see people performing specific actions. That's why action verbs are effective communicators. They throw the image up before your mind's eye.

If you ask yourself a simple question as you scan your sentences, your verbs will suddenly leap to life. Just ask: Who is doing what? Ask this every time you come to a nonaction verb. Your answer will show you how to rewrite the sentence or clause.

For example, take this notice in a research lab:

The adherence on the part of all technicians to adequate safety precautions is absolutely essential.

Where's the action verb? Nowhere. Who is doing what?

All technicians (*who*) must adhere to (*is doing*) adequate safety precautions (*what*).

110

The sentence is now more readable—but do you notice something? When you make it clear and simple, you can see how little it says! What are "adequate safety precautions"? How are the technicians supposed to "adhere to" them?

Separating the chaff from your writing will show you where you are being vague or unsure. Lots of gobbledygook can mask ignorance for a while, but at some point your reader is going to want to know what exactly you are saying. He'll like you a lot better if you know what you have to say and say it clearly and simply.

USE VERBS INSTEAD OF NOUNS

Now comes your final act of verbal alchemy. First you turned what you had written into what you meant. Then you turned abstract, impersonal statements into expressions of human action. Now you are going to give your phrases the elusive quality of *readability*. You're going to take away all the heavies and let your sentences flow, as your thoughts do. You are going to turn stodgy lumps of business language into a lively, interesting act of communication.

Don't forget, even if you become president of the company, you never have a captive audience. People may be forced to sit down with your memo in front of them—but no one can force them to take it in. Or want to act on it. Or admire you for it. They will do all these things, of their own accord, when you seek to fill their needs. And even if you have the worst possible task to ask of them, you can still fill some needs by writing an interesting, concerned memo in clear and simple language. You'll tell them what they want and need to know . . . you'll show your interest in them . . . and you will present it in language that pleases the mind.

We live, we work, we act, we meet, and sometimes we disagree. That's living! But write that expression in noun-ridden business phraseology, and you get:

> We are in existence, we are in employment, we take things into consideration, we take action on them, we have meetings, and on occasion we have disagreements.

Do you see what I mean? How much of your writing looks like that?

When you find a phrase consisting of a subject, a nonaction verb (to be, to have, to take, etc.) and an object, see if you can't turn it into a subject and verb instead. For instance:

we are in agreement	becomes	we agree
we shall make an examination of	becomes	we shall examine
I make mention of	becomes	I mention

this involves the necessity of	becomes	this requires
please take cognizance of	becomes	please note

Sometimes we find the right verb merely by looking at the noun (we are in *agree*ment = we *agree*). Other times you have to ask yourself the old question: What do I mean, in clear and simple language? You'll find out!

USE PREPOSITIONS INSTEAD OF PREPOSITIONAL PHRASES

Prepositional phrases weigh down sentences. They pile up such a lot of syllables to mean so little. Consider that *in order to, for the purpose of,* and *with a view to* all mean no more than—*to*! To prune your prose of excess prepositional foliage, look twice at *any phrase that starts and ends with a preposition.* Check to see if just one preposition would mean the same. If so, use it. Those extra words are wasted words. They can't justify their existence. Here are some examples:

along the lines *of*	=	like
in the matter *of*	=	about
in regard *to*	=	about, for
in the area *of*	=	in
on the part *of*	=	by
with reference *to*	=	about

Of course, there are times when you'll have to use a prepositional phrase. There isn't always a shorter, clearer substitute. But if you're filling up your pages with *in . . . of* and *with . . . to,* then that's all you are doing. Just filling up your pages.

WRITE ENGLISH

Finally, use English words. Real English words. The ones we use to talk to our friends.

That doesn't mean you should eschew all technical terms. If you were talking to a friend about the curative properties of salicylic acid, you would obviously call it salicylic acid. *But* you would say something like "We have been testing salicylic acid to see if it might relieve some arthritic pains." You would not say "The properties of salicylic acid have been under examination as to their potential capabilities for the relief of major and minor discomforts resulting from an arthritic condition."

112

You see?

By now, you can probably recognize much business jargon when you see it. Check back to Chapter 7 for a rundown on phony fancies and other assorted monstrosities. The outstanding quality of business jargon is its *fuzziness*. Words are piled up to diffuse, not detail, the picture. Clichés are so overused they can refer to almost anything. The writer says the same thing over and over and over again, using various redundancies and circumlocutions. Paradoxically, this uninspired repetition makes his message weaker than a single precise statement would be. The layers of tired expressions cover up the meaning, because they have been used so many times to mean so many things.

Here is a short list of the types of business jargon that can ruin your writing.

AVOID REDUNDANCIES

A redundancy is the use of two or more words when one would express the meaning perfectly well. For example:

- Unnecessary adjectives

  passing fad   *absolute* essentials

  ancient adage   *grave* danger

  complete satisfaction   *factual* truth

- Unnecessary prepositions or prepositional phrases

  attach *together*   large *in size*

  inside *of*   filled *to capacity*

  face *up to*   depreciate *in value*

  over *with*   pale *in color*

- Other notorious repeaters

  remove *completely*

  appear or seem *to be*

  continue to remain

  follow *after*

  divide *in two*

Of course there are many more. You can create them yourself! They all follow the same pattern: Write a word and then rob it of its power by adding another word with the same meaning. Don't do it.

CUT OUT CLICHÉS

A cliché is a once-colorful expression that has lost its eye-catching power through overuse. Clichés are the most frequent substitute for original thought. Here are some tired members of the businessperson's stable:

let's give it the acid test

we have agreed to disagree

it beggars description

give it the benefit of the doubt

that is the bone of contention

we have built-in safeguards

and by the same token

he has had a pretty checkered career

he is something of a diamond in the rough

that's a dynamite idea

this looks like an exercise in futility

we are caught between a rock and a hard place

will you give us a few well-chosen words?

that is definitely food for thought

going from the ridiculous to the sublime

we've got to iron out the difficulty here

it goes without saying

let's just keep our options open

that solution leaves much to be desired

I propose that we take the line of least resistance

... needs no introduction

this is of paramount importance

somebody's got to pay the piper

they were selling like hotcakes

we've got to stick to our guns and ...

in this day and age

from time immemorial

words fail to express ...

These words do indeed fail to express much of anything. They are the vaguest of vague indicators of the writer's thought, for two reasons. One, they have all been used so many times to mean so many things that they have degenerated into imprecise, impersonal catch-alls. Two, the writer himself rarely knows what they actually mean! What is a *bone* of contention? Are we talking Lassie-lingo? Why should a career be *checkered* and not patched? Have you ever formed a *line* of resistance? Did you ever take an *acid* test? Why should *hotcakes* sell any faster than waffles? What does *paramount* mean, exactly (besides the promise of a movie)? How do you *stick to a gun* — and why wouldn't you, if you had one?

Once you start taking clichés apart, a curious fact emerges. These expressions have little or nothing to do with you. They do not grow out of your personal experience. They are borrowed from another person who made a connection between one situation and another — in another place and time.

When you remark that they've got you "paying through the nose," you might as well say "They're overcharging me." The cliché adds nothing to that information, for it probably means nothing by itself to you or your reader. But the person who first used that expression meant something very specific indeed. In ancient times there was a poll tax in Sweden called a "nose tax." It was literally a penny per nose. If you don't know that—and if you don't mean to refer to that—the expression means nothing other than "I'm paying a lot." So why not either say what you mean or think up a meaningful analogy yourself? Clichés are nothing but padding. We use them to intensify our message — but all they do is blunt it. Avoid them.

THE FINAL CHECK

Once you have cleared up your message, any grammatical bloopers you may have left will leap out at you. Now that you're aware of the importance of the words you use and the way you put them together, you'll easily catch a faulty connection or a lapse of logic. Just check for:

- **faulty agreement of pronouns**
- **incorrectly placed punctuation marks**
- **the wrong preposition**

Then read your memo over once more. Is the tone respectful? Is the style interesting? Would you like to read it, if it came to you? Three times yes — and you're in business. Million-dollar business.

The million-dollar memo. It's not just words, words, words. By now, you will have gathered that the million-dollar memo is a written expression of trust in people. It comes from a person who really likes other people and who makes the conscious decision to treat them as well as he possibly can.

A person who says "Away with the pretenses and the bafflegab. We are people working together, not warring camps who use deceptions and subterfuge for survival. Let's *talk* to each other. Let's enjoy working together. Let's treat each other as we would like to be treated ourselves."

In your next memo, follow the golden rule:
Write unto others as you would have them write unto you.
Clearly. And simply. And with pleasure.
And you'll write a memo worth a million.

Epilogue
Language for the Fun of It

Perhaps this book has led you to suspect that, in all your years of busy business talk, you have been missing something. The sheer fun of language. The tremendous pleasure you can derive from using it in your own special, imaginative way. Once you're free of the need to hide behind words, you can actually start enjoying them. And your memos will be a clear and simple delight.

I'm going to give you a short list of further readings. It may give you a slight shock. You won't find the classic style books or business grammars here. I've told you what you need to know about grammar and style.

These ten readings will show you how to write.

If you get a copy of each of them—you'll have the best professional consultants within reach at all times. Most selections are less than one page.

1. A step-by-step, logical development of a concept:
"To be or not to be," Shakespeare (in *Hamlet,* Act II, Scene 2)

2. A vivid narration of an event:
"La Belle Dame Sans Merci," John Keats

3. Short, easy English words used for maximum power:
"Do Not Go Gentle Into That Good Night," Dylan Thomas

4. A wonderful exercise in description:
"Some Thoughts on the Common Toad," George Orwell

5. An effective ending:
"Father and Child," W. B. Yeats

6. Effective persuasion:
"To His Coy Mistress," Andrew Marvell

7. Calling for company sacrifice:
"Plan for saving 100,000 pounds," Benjamin Franklin (in *Poor Richard's Almanac*)

8. An admirable letter of complaint:
"To the Right Honorable Earl of Chesterfield," Samuel Johnson (in James Boswell, *The Life of Samuel Johnson*)

9. A trip report:
"The Inhabitants of Lilliput," Jonathan Swift (*Gulliver's Travels,* Chapter 6)

10. A reminder of the meaninglessness of business bafflegab: "Jabberwocky," Lewis Carroll (in *Through the Looking Glass*)

And remember Robert Frost—
But all the fun's in how you say a thing.